40 Days

To Freedom

Prayers and Proclamations
To Call Your Backslidden
Children Into Their Destiny

LaNora Van Arsdall

FountainGate Ministries Intl.

40 Days To Freedom

Prayers And Proclamations To Call Your Backslidden Children Into Their Destiny

© 2006 by LaNora Van Arsdall

Published by FountainGate Ministries Intl.
P.O. Box 1333
Gilbert, AZ 85299-1333
www.FountainGateIntl.org

Printed in the United States of America

ISBN: 978-0-9789394-0-3

Unless otherwise noted, Scripture is taken from the NEW AMERICAN STANDARD BIBLE ®. Copyright © The Lockman Foundation 1960, 1962, 1963, 1968, 1971, 1972, 1973, 1975, 1977, 1995.

DEDICATED TO:

I lovingly dedicate this book to my precious grandchildren:

Meshea and Riley
Noah and Emily
Anissa, Christian, and Zachary

May you always love Jesus and passionately serve Him. Besides Him, you are the greatest gift God ever gave me. I love you forever.

ACKNOWLEDGMENTS

My deepest gratitude to....

The Lord Jesus, my Beloved, who has patiently walked with me every step of the way. I have leaned upon You to help me come out of my wilderness wanderings and into Your promises. Thank You for Your unconditional, limitless love.

My two daughters, Melanie and Kari. God has used you to show me His ways in many things. I am so grateful for the privilege of being your mother and your friend. It blesses me to think that He would trust me with such precious treasures. You are each so unique and reflect Him in your own very special way. I love you forever!

My son-in-law, Timothy, who is also my pastor. Thank you for believing in me, praying for me, and urging me on. You have shown me the gentle and protective guidance of the Shepherd. Most of all thank you for loving Kari like Jesus loves her. And for being such a beautiful reflection of the Father's love to Noah and Emily...how that blesses me!

My son-in-law, Daniel, who is a precious, wise man of God, and a wonderful husband and father. You are a shining example of God's marvelous grace. Thank you for all your encouragement and prayers. God uses you to demonstrate His strength and care to me at just the right times. You are a gift of God to Melanie, the children, and to me.

My dearest friend, Barbara Boyd, who has prayerfully stood with me through every trial without judging me and rejoiced with me in every triumph. Thank you for your prayers and labor of love in typing and editing this book. You are a precious gem who reflects His heart. I am eternally grateful for your friendship.

Bama Spoon for all you did to make this book possible. Your servant's heart and attitude brings His special touch to each page. I thank God that you are part of the FountainGate staff and I am blessed to have you as my friend.

ACKNOWLEDGMENTS

Cathy Lowdermilk for your help in editing, your prayer support, and friendship. It so blessed me that even though you were in the middle of your doctoral thesis, you took time to help with this book. It is a joy to work together with you for His kingdom.

The entire FountainGate staff and board for your continual love, prayer support, and tireless labor for the Kingdom.

The staff and church family of Fountain of Life Fellowship. You are a true oasis in the desert. There's no place that I would rather be!

FOREWORD

When Mom told me of her new book, I was thrilled! I thought, "My God! No one has written of such things," – at least not this honestly. This subject has long been "off limits" with the exception of an occasional promise or encouraging word to "call home" the backslidden child. So, when I heard the vision of this book, my heart was ecstatic. I was that lost child once and because of His pursuing grace, and a mother who loved me unconditionally, I found my way back to Him.

Being a child who grew up in the ministry, I had witnessed a side of the church many never see. As I came into my college years, my perspective of life changed. I decided that there wasn't much in the church I wanted to be affiliated with. Even though I went through a spiritual crisis, I felt God there with me and speaking to me the entire time. My song has truly become "Where can I go from your Spirit?"

In my time of darkness and "finding myself," I came to know the unconditional love of my mother, which later translated into the unconditional love of my Heavenly Father. There were many nights of weeping and prayer as Mom and I poured out to each other. I was so surprised at her constant state of love. She never gave a religious, cookie-cutter answer when I would suggest my spiritual journey had left me jaded. There were times I also doubted God's existence. I wondered, if He did exist, how could He allow such injustice to come to me? I saw her pain at the choices I was making and the justification I used.

Amidst the peak of my searching, I could hear Mom's prayers. There's nothing like hearing Mom pray to sober you up! In my quest to know myself better, I quickly found the world had much less to offer than the church, even with all its weaknesses. It was Him I was in need of and nothing else. He showed me that the church I was rejecting was His church. I realized that I can't have Him and reject His family.

There were two things that impressed me the most during my dark times. One, Mom never let anyone speak evil of me. Two, her unconditional love was a true example of His character and love for me. I pray you find this book inspiring and freeing for you and your child. I am a living testimony of the miracle that He desires to create in you and through you. As a mom myself, I pray I can walk in the

FOREWORD

Godly heritage my mom started, and give to my children what was given to me – freedom!

Melanie Ross

It is my great privilege to write in the foreword for this book. I am living proof that what LaNora has written in these pages really does work! My name is Kari Thompson, LaNora's youngest daughter. I can remember countless occasions of my mother sitting in the living room waiting up late for me to come home. Somehow, she always knew everything I wasn't telling her.

I definitely had a season of running from God. I can look back and remember a shift that happened in my mom, a shift that began to shift me. This shift was brought about by strategic, heartfelt prayers! She had stopped trying to change me, and started letting Him. The Lord began coming after me in ways only a mother could dream.

I remember one time in the altars of my parents' church, an old friend of my mom's came and whispered in my ear, "You had better stop keeping me up nights praying for you, or I am going to start telling your mom what you are up to." This was someone who lived out of state and really hadn't been in contact with our family for quite sometime. Then, there was the time I woke up one morning, all of the sudden, disgusted at the sight or thought of the boy I had been dating for over a year. I ended it that day.

The Lord came after me through love songs on the radio, through teachers at school, and even through dreams. He captured my heart and ravished me with His love. I know that my eyes would have never truly opened had my mom not decided to go after God on my behalf. See, I know now that God was already pursuing me—but the enemy was too! Those strategic prayers accelerated the purposes of the Lord for me and pushed the enemy back.

My love story has become volumes since that time and I can see now how it really began when I was born in the heart of God. Today, I serve the Lord alongside my best friend and husband, Tim Thompson.

FOREWORD

We have given our lives to the Lord and are pastors for Fountain of Life Fellowship in Mesa, Arizona. We have two beautiful children and are passionately pursuing His presence for ourselves, our family, church, state, country and the world! Reader, dive into the journey of these pages and watch you and your family's lives be changed forever!!

Kari Thompson

INTRODUCTION

A Message to you from the author:

Throughout the years of ministry and travel, I discovered that countless numbers of parents were suffering silently over their backslidden children. Because of the accusations and condemnations of the devil and the judgments and opinions of men, they felt guilty and ashamed. My heart would go out to them as they would share their grief in the altar and ask for prayer. Little did I know that one day, I would be the parent with the same problem. Both of my daughters had their times of backsliding. I felt so disqualified and responsible. My heart would break over and over again. Believe me when I tell you... I tried everything!

Through it all, I learned that there is no formula. However, there are strategies that come from time spent in the presence of the Lord. This devotional was born out of my own desperation for my children's freedom. Through the inspiration and direction of the Holy Spirit, I learned secrets to unlock their destinies and secure their future in God. It is my deepest desire to pass these secrets on to you, my friend. If what I learned can save you even one moment of unnecessary agony, I will have fulfilled the mandate that God gave me.

I do not pretend to have all the answers and I humbly confess that I failed many times through the process. Yet, in God's wonderful grace, I found His Word and ways to be flawless. "40 Days to Freedom" is a journey of one day at a time. I am praying that you will receive the word of the Lord each day that will bring you into new levels of healing and freedom and will give you personal direction for the liberation of your children.

The battle has raged on long enough! Your children have a calling on their lives and it is time for them to be free from the snares of the enemy. You, as their parent, carry an authority and an anointing to unlock the prison doors.

This book is more than just information. It is going to release an impartation from God that will bring an increase to the authority and anointing that you already possess. I have been releasing these truths wherever I go and have seen numerous parents set free from the shame

INTRODUCTION

and humiliation that has tormented them. As well, I have received many praise reports of their children coming back to the Lord.

There were times in my personal journey that I didn't know if I could make it another day. I didn't have a drop of faith to lean on. But, I had a friend who said, "You can lean on my faith today." What sweet relief that was! If you have one of those days, just pick up this devotional and lean on mine. I believe your children are on their way home. Together we will rejoice and give to God all the glory!

Watching expectantly with you,

LaNora

Day 1
Called By His Name, Created For His Glory

They are not yours. They are His.

Isaiah 43:5-7 *"'Do not fear for I am with you. I will bring your offspring from the east and gather them from the west. I will say to the north 'Give them up!' and to the south, 'Do not hold them back.' Bring MY sons from afar, and MY daughters from the ends of the earth, everyone who is called by MY name, and whom I have created for MY GLORY, whom I have formed, even whom I have made.'"*

What is your worst fear about your children, my friend? Have you imagined in the dark of the night, that your phone may ring with the most tragic news? Maybe you have awakened suddenly at some late hour and realized your son or daughter still wasn't home. Your mind begins to race, "Where is he? What could he be doing? Is she in a dark alley somewhere?" On and on the fearful thoughts flood into the night without mercy. It is in that moment of deepest darkness and gripping fear that you must choose. You may not be able to find your faith because your feelings have swallowed it up like a tsunami wave. Right then, you must remember this important fact:

They are not yours. They are His.

With that in mind, begin to yield to the Inner Voice of the One who called them by His name before you ever thought of them. Yes, He has His purposes for your offspring and He will bring His glorious plans out of the deepest depths and from the farthest distance. Let His voice arise from your wounded heart. You will be surprised how such authority can thunder forth from a broken, but yielded vessel.

Prayer:

Father, I feel so afraid sometimes that__(Name)__ will _____ (name your fear). I am sorry that I can't find the faith to overcome the fear sometimes. And, so, I need You to call Your child into full salvation and restoration to Your purposes. I lay him/her into Your arms and care. Please reach where I cannot reach. He/She is **Yours** called by **Your** name and created for **Your** glory. Glorify Your Name!

12

Called By His Name, Created For His Glory

Proclamation:

In Jesus' powerful name, I declare that my offspring are being gathered from afar. Every place that they are being held captive, I say to you, "Give them up! DO NOT hold them back! **They are God's children, called by His name and created for His glory!**"

Day 2
The Double Portion!

Hold your head high and enforce Calvary's victory for yourself and your children.

Isaiah 61:6-7; 9 *"But you will be called the priests of the Lord; you will be spoken of as ministers of our God. You will eat the wealth of nations and in their riches you will boast.* **Instead of your shame you will have a double portion and instead of humiliation they will shout for joy over their portion.** *Therefore they will possess* **a double portion in their land.** *Everlasting joy will be theirs...Then their offspring will be known among the nations and their descendants in the midst of the peoples. All who see them will recognize them because* **they are the offspring whom the Lord has blessed!***"

What do you say to people when they ask about your kids? What are you supposed to say anyway? Sometimes people, though they may be well-meaning (or just nosey), make a painful situation worse with their probing questions. Somehow you feel it is up to you to "cover" or to defend why your son/daughter isn't at church or the family holiday gathering. Or maybe you struggle to justify their "style" as a "phase" they are going through. You can literally feel the eyes of the onlookers trying to "discern." If your child does come to church, you may find yourself praying, "God, please don't let anyone say or do anything that will turn him off!" In the meantime, you become distracted by his folded arms or that he rolls his eyes with boredom and possibly disgust. You leave church services exhausted from holding your breath and you feel relieved that it's over.

Sound familiar? You have been under reproach, shame, and humiliation. You may feel so disqualified and disgraced by your obvious failure – "How could you ever have anything to say or do for the Lord as long as your own child is such a mess?" – the accuser says repeatedly in your ears.

My question for you today is: Is your identity bound to the behavior of your son or daughter? Or is your identity hidden in Calvary's cross? Have you died to your reputation yet? It seems that the Holy Spirit is teaching you one of God's secrets through your child. Jesus made Himself of no reputation and endured the shame of the cross for the

14

joy that was set before Him (see Heb. 12:2). Jesus, Himself, already paid the price for the shame of sin sickness. *"Surely our griefs He Himself bore, and our sorrows (pains) He carried"* (Isaiah 53:4). Since He has paid the price of disgrace, the best thing you can possibly do is:

Hold your head high and enforce Calvary's victory for yourself and your children.

The "instead of" is where you must stand. Position yourself in the anointing and its authority – the kind that gives you *"beauty* **instead** *of ashes and the oil of joy* **instead of** *mourning"* (Isaiah 61:3). **Instead of** shame – a double portion! **Instead of** humiliation – a shout of everlasting joy!

Once my Father said to me, *"I was the perfect parent, and My son, Adam, still fell."* That puts it in perspective, dear one. Regardless of your parenting successes or failures, your children have a choice. He went on to say, *"If you won't take the blame now, then you won't touch the glory later."* So, today, you must release the responsibility for their decisions and choices and receive a double portion of His presence and power. The devil knows if he can keep you defeated with shame and condemnation you will not be able to make your freedom stand. It's time for a new identity – a new look for the new day.

Prayer:

Lord Jesus, thank You for bearing my shame and reproach and that of my children. Please cleanse and forgive me for living under the old nature and identity and carrying the burden of responsibility for my children's choices. Set me free from this pattern of trying to take Your place as their Savior. Hallelujah! Glorify Your Name – not mine.

Proclamation:

In the anointing of the Holy Spirit and the authority of His Name, Jesus, I boldly renounce all shame and humiliation and break its power over my life and my children's lives. I enforce the victory of Calvary and proclaim that the double portion belongs to me and to my children. We are the priests of the Lord and the ministers of God. And **together** we shall shout for joy over our portion.

Day 3
Divine Intervention

> *Let Him touch the untouchable and change the unchangeable.*

Luke 7:13-15 *"And when the Lord saw her, He felt compassion for her, and said to her, 'Do not weep.' And He came up and touched the coffin; and the bearers came to a halt. And He said, 'Young man, I say to you, arise!' And the dead man sat up and began to speak. And Jesus gave him back to his mother."*

It is such an awesome and comforting truth to know that Jesus feels compassion for us. He is moved by your tears. He knows that the odds are apparently insurmountable from your view point. He doesn't rebuke you for your unbelief. He simply walks into the midst of your misery. He gently whispers, "Do not weep." He begins to minister to your pain and broken heart – even before He performs the miracle you have longed for.

By just one touch, He stopped the bearers of the coffin of the widow's only son. Somehow, the friends of the dead boy recognized the authority in His voice. The procession of death was halted because the One who was Life stepped in. The other religious leaders would have refused to touch the coffin because it would be considered unclean according to the Law. But this rabbi was different. His amazing love was greater and weightier than the traditions of men. He even interrupted the young man's peers as they carried him away for burial. Peer pressure can sometimes be the death march for our children. Yet, the Lord was intercepting what seemed to be the inevitable. Speaking to the lifeless corpse, He called for the boy's arising. The young man sat up and began to speak. (I wonder what he said!) Jesus gave him back to his mother.

Whether your son or daughter is being carried away by their peers or is simply walking away from their future and family because they want to, the answer is the same. Jesus is coming into the midst of the death procession to perform a miracle.

Let Him touch the untouchable and change the unchangeable!

Divine Intervention

He is not intimidated by the severity of the problem. Is it addictions, immoralities, wrong relationships, agnosticism, atheism, or the occult? He will reach where you cannot reach and go where you cannot go. There are **no limits** for Him. And…He has perfect timing. What may seem "too late" to you is the perfect setting for Him. It wouldn't be a miracle if it weren't impossible!

Prayer:

Precious Lord Jesus, please heal my broken heart. Only You can cause the tears to stop flowing. I acknowledge my desperate need for Your divine intervention. Please step into the midst of _____(Name's)_____ procession of death and raise him/her up. And, would You put him/her back into my arms again? Thank You for Your compassion towards us. Glorify Your Name!

Proclamation:

In the mighty name of Jesus, I set myself in agreement with His word. To the death procession of __(Name)__ I say: "Halt! You shall go no further!" I speak to the power of peer pressure: "Be broken!" To my son/daughter, I say to you: "Arise into your purpose and calling!"

Day 4
Let His Kingdom Come!

There is a position in Him that puts it all in perspective.

Isaiah 46: 9-10 *"'...I am God and there is no other. I am God and there is no one like Me,* **Declaring the end from the beginning** *and from ancient times things which have not been done, saying,* **My purpose will be established,** *and I will accomplish all My good pleasure.'"*

His name is Alpha and Omega, Beginning and End, First and the Last, Author and Finisher. You can rejoice, dear friend, in the knowledge that He is committed to your son's/daughter's purpose. He is **so** committed that He has already declared the finished product! He cried out from Calvary's cross, **"It is finished!"** Before ___(Name)___ was formed in the womb, God formed his/her purpose and established His will to be deposited deep in your child's heart.

When that piercing cry rang out from Calvary, the earth quaked, rocks split, the veil in the temple was rent, and tombs were opened. Jesus, our Intercessor, was stretched out between the sin and darkness of earth and the glory and purity of heaven. Yes, He was in the gap between the awful reality of your son's/daughter's condition and circumstance and his/her divine purpose and destiny. It was a place you could never fill – the space between what is and what shall be. Jesus, the Author and Finisher, paid the price for your child's purpose. That price is sufficient to cause the world's effects to shake, the hard rocky places to be broken up, the veil of deception to be rent, and the dead to be raised – Yes, the dead raised!

So, where does this leave you? What can be done to cause the truth of heaven to invade the life of your offspring and set him/her on course with their life's purpose? Because Jesus has now been *"...seated in heavenly places far above all rule and authority and power and domain, and every name that is named, not only in this age, but in the age to come ..."* (Ephesians 1:20-21), He issues forth the divine decree and declares the completed work before it has even begun. Therefore, it is to our advantage to be positioned there with Him (Ephesians 2:6). To Abraham *"it was reckoned to him as righteousness that he called those things that were not as though they already were"* (Romans 4:3).

18

Let His Kingdom Come!

I am not speaking to you of a formula of "name it and claim it." Nor am I telling you to ignore the obvious. I am sharing with you a secret that I have learned: There is a higher way to look at things.

There is a position in Him
that puts it all in perspective.

From that position, the victory of Calvary is enforced and the kingdom of heaven is established on earth. From the seat of government, a verdict is rendered on the unjust trespassing of the enemy upon the life of your seed.

Because of your God-given authority as the parent, you have a spiritual right to enforce the kingdom of heaven and His will on your earth (the place of your designated dominion). You must begin to send forth the word of heaven's perspective over your son or daughter. By so doing, you are exercising your legal right as God's designated authority on the earth. You will find this type of "enforcing" to be more effective and powerful than all the words of pleading, reasoning or threatening you may have used to try and convince your child of the call and purpose of God on their life.

May His Kingdom come and His will be done on earth – as it is in heaven!

Prayer:

Father, please forgive me for living in the earthly perspective rather than the heavenly position You have given me through Christ Jesus. Please, teach me, Holy Spirit, how to perceive and proclaim God's will. Thank You for the finished work of Calvary and the power of Your blood. In Jesus' wonderful name, Amen.

Proclamation:

Because of the authority given to me as a parent by the courts of heaven, I now decree in agreement with God's word: _____(Name)_____ **is** saved, delivered, and healed. He/She **is** moving in the fullness of his/her calling. I enforce the victory of the cross over his/her life and say:"It is finished!" **No more** of the world and its influence controlling him/her! **No more** rocky hard places blocking his/her ability to receive the Word of God! **No more** veil of deception – but the Sword of the Spirit now rends the veil! **No more** death and destruction!

Day 5
Treasures of Darkness

> *You must lay aside the "if onlys," see with the eye of faith, and dig for treasure with God.*

Isaiah 45:2-3 *"' I will go before you and make the rough places smooth, I will shatter the doors of bronze, and cut through their iron bars. And I will give you the treasures of darkness, and hidden wealth of secret places, in order that you may know that it is I, the Lord, the God of Israel, who calls you by your name.'"*

There isn't a prison so fortified or a dungeon so deep that it cannot be overtaken by the love, presence and power of God. Buried deep in the darkness and hidden behind the thick stone walls lies a treasure. Somewhere in there is someone you once knew – someone full of life and wide-eyed innocence. Someone whose hair you used to stroke with a gentle touch. Someone who ran to you as soon as their knee was scraped to get you to kiss the "owie." What happened to that little boy/girl? It's as if it were another lifetime ago when you remember that little one snug in the bed down the hall. Somehow the security and safety of your love wasn't enough to hold them steady when life threw the curve ball. You have spent way too much time trying to figure it out and way too many hours and energy rehearsing what you could have done differently. The words, "If only".... begins the descent into your sleepless nights of regrets.

But, now, just when I almost gave up all hope, I see a glimpse of a glistening something in the distance. Peeking through the iron prison bars, I can see a little glimmer of familiarity. I think I can see a hint of my precious baby girl. Can you see yours? It's the little sparkle here and there that lets us know God is moving. Some people call it "grasping at straws" but I call it digging with God for treasure. If you will just look through the eye of faith –much like a miner can see the diamonds in the rocks – you will see that a process is taking place. It may not look like much to you but God is working in the hidden places.

Later on your son/daughter will tell you the things you didn't know. Like the time he had the dream from God or the angelic visitation. He/She will tell you of the times he was saved out of serious danger by the hand of the Lord. You will hear the stories of people (God's secret agents) who were brought across their path to help them find their way back, but for now...

*You must lay aside the "if onlys," see with
the eye of faith, and dig for treasure with God.*

He promises to give you the treasures of darkness. Out of the rubble a testimony is forming – not only your son's/daughter's testimony – but yours!

Prayer:

Lord, I need You to go before me into the darkness of __(Name)__.   Make the way where I can see no way. Give me the eye of faith so I can see into that invisible place and believe You for the impossible! Thank You for the anointing to open prison doors and set my captive one free. Glorify Your Name! Amen.

Proclamation:

__(Name)__, I speak to the treasure within you to come forth – the deposit of God's word and nature, and calling – to break out of the darkness. I send the light of His word into your midst right now. I command the rocks to break open and the prison doors to swing wide! __(Name)__, let the darkness be split by the brightness of His glory. It is time for you to shine! In Jesus' powerful name – **Break Through and Break Out!**

Day 6
The Battle Is Not Yours!

> **The battle is not yours but God's.**

2 Chron. 20:15, 17-18, 22 *"'...Do not fear or be dismayed because of this great multitude, for the battle is not yours but God's...You need not fight in this battle; station yourselves, stand and see the salvation of the Lord on your behalf, O Judah and Jerusalem. Do not fear or be dismayed, tomorrow go out to face them, for the Lord is with you.'*
Jehoshaphat bowed his head with his face to the ground and all Judah and the inhabitants of Jerusalem fell down before the Lord, worshiping the Lord...And when they began singing and praising, the Lord set ambushes..."

Perhaps the fears and anxieties have paralyzed you and you may feel that all your strength is gone. You can't muster up one more prayer. You can't even think of another prayer to pray. The enemies of your soul have surrounded and outnumbered you. You feel like giving up, but then you think, "If I don't fight, who will? If I don't pray, then who will?" So, you try again. The prayers seem feeble and powerless. Nothing seems to be changing. You may try fasting and end up frustrated (and hungry). Your heart is breaking again and again. Desperately, you cry out to God that nothing is working!

When the enemy surrounded Jehoshaphat, the king of Judah, he prayed this prayer: *"...For we are powerless before this great multitude who are coming against us, nor do we know what to do, but our eyes are on Thee"* (2 Chron. 20:12). Jehoshaphat admitted to God that he did not know what to do.

It was a liberating moment for the king. There he stood – a man of power and authority – powerless. If anyone should have known what to do, it should have been him. When he surrendered his position of power and turned his eyes to God, the strategy of heaven was released to him. The Spirit of the Lord spoke an unusual word to him through the prophet. The prophet declared,

> *"It's not your battle – it's God's! All you need to do is stand and see what He will do."*

23

The Battle Is Not Yours!

That strategy really goes against our way of thinking, doesn't it? After all, aren't we the ones who gave birth to and raised these kids all of these years? You've always fixed the problem, had the answer, corrected the mistakes and even covered up their sin – so no one would think badly of them (or you). Now it seems that God is saying, "It's My turn." Since you don't know what to do, maybe He is going to take on this battle for you. Could it be that He can see that you are at the end of your strength? I think so. Lovingly, He is sending you a message from heaven today. *"You need not fight in this battle; station yourself, stand and see the salvation of the Lord on your behalf."*

Your role, this time, is simple. Worship the Lord. Praise the Lord. Thank Him. Bow before Him. Love Him. Adore Him. And…Watch Him!

Prayer:

Lord, today, I admit my sense of powerlessness, my lack of strength and strategy and my great need for You. I turn my eyes upon You and wait for You and Your salvation. In Jesus' precious name, Amen.

Proclamation:

I give thanks and praise You, Lord. You made the heavens and the earth, the sea and the depths. You made __(Name)__ and I thank You for his/her deliverance. Give me a new song of praise to sing to You and over my kids. Hallelujah!

Day 7
A Day To Praise

Today is a special day! Today is set aside to praise God and give Him thanks for all He has done, for all He is doing, and for all He is going to do. The Lord is enthroned upon your praises and your enemies will be confused. Use these scriptures to help you spend the day in praise.

Ps. 47:1-2 *"O clap your hands, all peoples; shout to God with the voice of joy. For the Lord Most High is to be feared, a great King over all the earth."*

Ps. 96:1-5 *"Sing to the Lord a new song; sing to the Lord, all the earth. Sing to the Lord, bless His name; proclaim good tidings of His salvation from day to day. Tell of His glory among the nations, His wonderful deeds among all the peoples. For great is the Lord, and greatly to be praised; He is to be feared above all gods. For all the gods of the peoples are idols, but the Lord made the heavens."*

Ps. 100:1-5 *"Shout joyfully to the Lord, all the earth. Serve the Lord with gladness; come before Him with joyful singing. Know that the Lord Himself is God; it is He who has made us, and not we ourselves; we are His people and the sheep of His pasture. Enter His gates with thanksgiving, and His courts with praise. Give thanks to Him; bless His name. For the Lord is good; His lovingkindness is everlasting, and His faithfulness to all generations."*

Ps. 150 *"Praise the Lord! Praise God in His sanctuary; praise Him in His mighty expanse. Praise Him for His mighty deeds. Praise Him according to His excellent greatness. Praise Him with trumpet sound; praise Him with harp and lyre. Praise Him with timbrel and dancing; praise Him with stringed instruments and pipe. Praise Him with loud cymbals; praise Him with resounding cymbals. Let everything that has breath praise the Lord. Praise the Lord!"*

Acts 16:25-26 *"But about midnight Paul and Silas were praying and singing hymns of praise to God, and the prisoners were listening to them; and suddenly there came a great earthquake, so that the foundations of the prison house were shaken; and immediately all the doors were opened, and everyone's chains were unfastened."*

Day 8
It Is Well

> **Shut the door and watch what He will do.**

2 Kings 4:20-21, 23 *"When he had taken him and brought him to his mother, he sat on her lap until noon, and then died. And she went up and laid him on the bed of the man of God, and shut the door behind him and went out... And he* (her husband*) said, 'Why will you go to him* (Elisha, the man of God) *today? It is neither new moon nor Sabbath.' And she said, 'It will be well.'"*

2 Kings 4:25-26 *"...Behold, yonder is the Shunamite. Please run now to meet her and say to her, 'Is it well with you? Is it well with your husband? Is it well with the child?' And she answered, 'It is well.'"*

2 Kings 4:30 *"And the mother of the lad said, 'As the Lord lives and as you yourself live, I will not leave you.' And he* (Elisha) *arose and followed her."*

The young man's birth was a miracle that the Shunamite woman had not expected. Just a few years earlier, even though barren, she had found a sense of fulfillment in serving the man of God whenever he would pass by. She and her husband had built a special upper chamber as an addition to their home for the prophet. The woman enjoyed showing hospitality to Elisha and expected nothing in return. Then, one day, her life changed forever. She received a prophecy, a promise of a child. In one year's time, she was a mother of a beautiful baby boy. Becoming a mother or father changes everything, doesn't it? Your life is no longer your own. Your time, energy, money and **heart** now belong to this tiny new life. And...as you know, that's just the beginning.

There came a day that the baby became a young man (where did the time go?), and he went into the field to work with his father. He began to complain of the pain in his head and so his father sent him back to the house. There, his mother held him until he died. Struggling, the woman carried her son to the upper chamber, laid him on the prophet's bed, and shut the door. As the servant saddled the donkey for her, she told her husband, "I am going to the man of God!" Her husband wondered about the sudden trip since it was not a special holiday or time of religious observance. She simply told him, "It will be well."

It Is Well

When the prophet saw her coming, he sent his servant to meet her. The messenger questioned her as to the condition of her family. Her response was the same... "It is well." Yet, when she reached the man of God, she fell at his feet and refused to let go, unless he came with her. The story has a happy ending. The man of God followed the woman back to her home, entered the upper room, shut the door and revived her son. Then he gave him back to his mother.

I wonder as she frantically drove the donkey to Elisha's location if she thought, "Why did God give me this son, only to take him away? Is this some kind of cruel joke?" I don't know what she thought, but I do know what she said. We would be wise to learn from her – what to say while we pursue our miracle. What you say actually depends on **who** you are saying it to. To her husband and to the prophet's servant she said, "It is well." Was she lying or was she proclaiming? Could it be that she discerned what information the two could handle? Or could it be that she knew her own heart? Maybe she knew what effect their responses could have on her own shaky faith.

When she reached the prophet, she spilled it all. No fancy words, no spiritual protocols, just a basic, desperate, "HELP!" and also a very sincere "Why?"

Sometimes, it is like that – no more words to say...just, "HELP!" All of the times you have said, "It is well" to those who asked, have been noted by God. He actually considers your times of "staying in faith" as a vote of confidence. But today, you are at His feet. Say whatever you need to. He can handle your rawest emotions. But, then, bring Him home with you into the very midst of the disappointments and dashed dreams.

Shut the door and watch what He will do.

Prayer:

My Father, please help me to discern who can hear my deepest heart's cry and agree with me for my child. Lord, help me to proclaim, "It is well" at the times my soul is fainting. Lead me quickly to Your presence. In Jesus' name, Amen.

It Is Well

Proclamation:

Before heaven and earth, I proclaim, in Jesus' name and because of His presence and power, "It is well!"

Day 9
Deliver Us From Evil!

> *He will take whatever belief you do have and multiply it into a miracle.*

Mark 9:21-24 *"And He asked his father, 'How long has this been happening to him?' And he said, 'From childhood. And it has often thrown him both into the fire and into the water to destroy him. But if you can do anything, take pity on us and help us!' And Jesus said to him, 'If you can? All things are possible to him who believes.' Immediately the boy's father cried out and began saying, 'I do believe, help my unbelief!'"*

The boy's father had brought his tormented son to the disciples to be delivered. They were unsuccessful. Possibly, you have done the same thing – brought (or shall I say dragged) your child to various ministers and special services. You have hoped if you could just get him/her to the right place at the right time…maybe it would all change. It is more than disappointing when the only effect the anointing of that minister has is to agitate and upset your backslidden one. The demonic spirits take advantage of the apparent failure of the minister or the church to be able to bring the needed breakthrough. You helplessly watch as the enemy of your soul exploits the one you love and wreaks havoc with their life. Your son or daughter may not literally convulse, fall into the fire or the water, or foam at the mouth – but the repetition of the destructive behaviors breaks your heart just the same.

"Will this ever end? Will the devil continue to attack until there is nothing left of my precious child? Can't anyone do something?" All of these questions and more flood your soul. You call everyone you know, seek advice, and try spiritual formulas offered by sympathetic, well-meaning ministers. There is no amount of money that you would not spend or distance you would not travel to gain the deliverance of your son/daughter. You secretly wish it could be you instead of your child being tormented day and night. Maybe you even tried to make a deal with the devil. It's amazing what we will do for our kids.

This father was at the end of his rope when he brought his son to Jesus. He said, **"If** You can do anything…" He said "if" to the Word, Himself, the One who was the creator of the universe. The One, who walked out on nothing and with a word spoke the worlds into existence, stood before the failing faith of a father. "If" is a big word – everything hinges on it – possibility and impossibility. The "if" is not too big to Jesus. Your lack of faith doesn't surprise or offend Him. He knows you're tired. He knows you've given your best effort and that you have run out of options. It's okay.

He will take whatever belief you do have
and multiply it into a miracle.

Go ahead and give Him just a little something to work with. Does He need it? No, but you do. You need to be part of your child's deliverance. Right now, tell Him what you do believe. He will take it from there. If you listen carefully, you will hear Him saying, "All things are possible!"

Prayer:

Lord, I have tried everything I know to try. I have taken _____(Name)_____ to all kinds of ministers and meetings. No one and nothing has helped. I don't understand and my faith wavers. So today, Lord, I want You to know that I do believe. Yet, I still need Your help to overcome my unbelief. Thank You for Your love, patience and mercy toward me. Be glorified! Amen!

Proclamation:

_____(Name)_____, I bring you before Jesus today to receive your deliverance. Jesus, I believe that You shall do the impossible. _____(Name)_____, be delivered! Be set free! No more shall the destructive works of Satan be wreaking havoc in our lives! I stand upon the desire of God for my child's full deliverance from all works of darkness. Hallelujah!

Day 10
Sow In Tears

> To God, tears are seeds – seeds of your heart. You may think that they are wasted, but actually they are worship.

Ps. 56:8-9 *"Thou hast taken account of my wanderings, put my tears in Thy bottle; are they not in Thy book? Then my enemies will turn back in the day when I call; this I know, that God is for me."*

Ps. 126:5 *"Those who sow in tears shall reap with joyful shouting."*

Luke 7:38 *"...and standing behind Him at His feet, weeping, she began to wet His feet with her tears, and kept wiping them with the hair of her head, and kissing His feet, and anointing them with the perfume."*

Did you know that God keeps track of your every tear? He even records the words that you cannot express. He is a master of detail and is intimately acquainted with your anxious thoughts. I am glad that God can read my mind. He knows what I really mean when I say what I say. It is good to know there is Someone who truly does understand me without a word being uttered.

To God, tears are seeds – seeds of your heart. You may think that they are wasted, but actually they are worship.

You are worshiping Him every time you turn your child over to Him. You are worshiping when you choose His way of doing things. You are worshiping when you get up on Sunday morning and go to church when you feel like crawling back under your covers. You are worshiping when you cry out to Him instead of turning to something or someone else to make you feel better.

Every tear that rolls down your cheek is counted as worship when you remain faithful to God and His Word regardless of how things appear. It isn't easy to worship when you know what others are thinking and saying. Perhaps you feel judged or you feel your son or daughter is being judged. Yet, when you worship in the valley of weeping, it is a sweet fragrance to Him.

Sow In Tears

Jesus said that when a kernel (or seed) of wheat falls in the ground, that it must die in order to bring forth fruit. But, a heart seed is different...it ascends to heaven and is stored in God's tear bottle. That moment is recorded in heaven's book. Just as a natural kernel or seed reproduces itself in the fruit, so a tear reproduces itself in the form of rain. That rain brings forth the harvest. The harvest brings forth...joy!

When the woman brought the expensive ointment to anoint Jesus, she wept and she worshiped. It was the combination of ingredients that He loved. The others considered her act of passionate worship as a waste; but He called it precious.

The next time you begin to weep over your backslidden offspring, consider worshiping Him at the same time. Don't waste your sorrows on pity parties. If you worship with your tears, you will be planting heavenly seeds that will result in the rain of His presence falling upon your child's life. And the harvest...is full of rejoicing!

Prayer:

Lord, I ask You to please remind me that You are here with me when I cry. Help me to remember that I am not alone. Holy Spirit, cause me to arise to worship when I feel like quitting. I am looking forward to Your rain. Thank You for making my tears count. I love You.

Proclamation:

Spend this time simply worshiping the Lord. Worship is a declaration of God's will and kingdom being established on earth. Consider lifting your son's or daughter's picture before the Lord as you give Him all the praise for the coming harvest and joy!

Day 11
A Day To Be Healed

This is a day to receive a special touch from the Lord. He desires to minister a healing word to you and bring you into a new dimension of wholeness. When our children are away from the Lord, many times we experience extreme stress which may cause our bodies to suffer with sickness, disease, or various aches and pains. Our emotions may be wounded because of our heartbreak. He can heal your body and your soul as you come into His presence today. As you meditate upon His Word, let Jesus touch you wherever you may be hurting or suffering today.

3 John 2 *"Beloved, I pray that in all respects you may prosper and be in good health, just as your soul prospers."*

Isa. 53:4-5 (Amplified) *"Surely He has borne our griefs (sicknesses, weaknesses, and distresses) and carried our sorrows and pains [of punishment], yet we (ignorantly] considered Him stricken, smitten, and afflicted by God [as if with leprosy]. But He was wounded for our transgressions, He was bruised for our guilt and iniquities; the chastisement [needful to obtain] peace and well-being for us was upon Him, and with the stripes [that wounded] Him we are healed and made whole."*

Ex. 15:26 *"And He said, 'If you will give earnest heed to the voice of the Lord your God, and do what is right in His sight, and give ear to His commandments, and keep all His statutes, I will put none of the diseases on you which I have put on the Egyptians; for I, the Lord, am your healer.'"*

Ps. 103:1-5 *"Bless the Lord, O my soul; and all that is within me, bless His holy name. Bless the Lord, O my soul, and forget none of His benefits; who pardons all your iniquities; who heals all your diseases; who redeems your life from the pit; who crowns you with lovingkindness and compassion; who satisfies your years with good things, so that your youth is renewed like the eagle."*

Ps. 147:3 *"He heals the brokenhearted, and binds up their wounds."*

Matt. 8:16-17 *"And when evening had come, they brought to Him many who were demon-possessed; and He cast out the spirits with a* *word, and healed all who were ill in order that what was spoken through Isaiah the prophet might be fulfilled, saying, 'He Himself took our infirmities, and carried away our diseases.'"*

Day 12
Welcome Home!

> *"If you will stop feeding her, she will realize she is in the pig pen."*

Luke 15:13-17a *"And not many days later, the younger son gathered everything together and went on a journey into a distant country, and there he squandered his estate with loose living. Now, when he had spent everything, a severe famine occurred in that country and he began to be in need. And he went and attached himself to one of the citizens of that country, and he sent him into his fields to feed swine. And he was longing to fill his stomach with the pods that the swine were eating, and no one was giving anything to him. But when he came to his senses, he said..."*

Luke 15:20 *"And he got up and came to his father. But while he was still a long way off, his father saw him, and felt compassion for him, and ran and embraced him, and kissed him."*

Prodigal: spending recklessly; reckless extravagance; one who spends recklessly; wasteful; extravagant waste (Dictionary.com).

I remember the exact spot I was standing when God set me free. There in my friend's kitchen I finally got it settled. Her kitchen island became my personal altar. I had turned our friendly conversation down the same path of despair. I always seemed to say at least something about my prodigal daughter. It didn't matter what the topic had been, it would always end up here. I couldn't seem to ever have her off my mind and heart. So, out of the abundance of my overwhelmed heart, my mouth would speak. I would usually regret it and felt sorry that I couldn't go a day without the subject coming up. I really couldn't help myself. It was always there – the knots in my stomach – the tightness in my chest. There seemed to be a foreboding threat, from the devil, hanging over my head like a dark cloud. I felt myself braced for bad or tragic news every day. The stress in my body was unreal and was having serious effects on my health.

That day when my friend spoke the truth to me, I was set free. She said, "Your daughter is eating just enough from your table to not realize she's starving to death."

Welcome Home!

"If you will stop feeding her, she will realize she is in the pig pen."

How was I "feeding her?" you may ask. I was giving her a scripture here and a testimony there. I would tell her what God was doing and about the good services she was missing. Sometimes, she would call me in the midst of a crisis and ask me to find out for her what God was saying and I would do that too. She would get in messes and I would bail her out every time. I thought it was love. I thought it was the right thing to do. And, sometimes, it was. But, mostly, it relieved God's pressure and delayed her homecoming. She had all the privileges of the Father's house without the responsibilities that come with the position of being His child. She didn't know she was in the pig pen.

I left my kitchen altar that day knowing I would have to let her starve. I would have to let her waste her inheritance until she spent everything. I never told her that I was doing anything differently. I'm not even sure if she noticed. But, I knew that I was no longer her "savior." She then began to realize that she had need. It wasn't easy to watch her go deeper into the mire. But one day, she came to her senses. I don't really know what her final straw was. All I know is…that I lifted my eyes and saw her coming home from a far distant land. The "citizen" that she had attached herself to in the foreign country didn't give up and let go of her easily. After all, he loved her. He benefited from her backslidings and was actually attracted to her anointing.

It was quite a journey for her to come home. It wasn't a "suddenly." It was a process. However, as she came into view, I dropped everything and ran down the road to meet her. So, this is a story of two people's freedom – mine and hers! Once, I truly let go of the spiritual controls of her life, He took hold, brought her to her senses, and pulled her out of the pit. Hallelujah!

Today, she is one of my best friends. Many times she is the one giving me wise advice. She doesn't do everything the way I think she should and she is not a cookie cutter version of me. She is who she is. She looks more and more like Him. And so do I.

Welcome Home!

Prayer:

Father, please help me to stop "feeding" ____(Name)____. I let go of the spiritual controls of his/her life and repent for trying to be the "savior." You are the only One he/she needs. You are the only One who can satisfy. Please forgive me and set me free from this sin of spiritual pride. In Jesus' name, our Savior, Amen.

Proclamation:

____(Name)____, I send you the word of freedom. I say to you, "Come to your senses! Get up out of the mire! Detach from every wrong attachment! Come home to the Father's house! We are watching, waiting, and expecting your homecoming."

Day 13
Only Believe

Interruptions and delays are not a problem to Jesus. Bad news or an evil report doesn't hinder Him one bit.

Mark 5:36 *"But Jesus, overhearing what was being spoken said to the synagogue official, 'Do not be afraid any longer, only believe'* (literally: keep on believing)."

Jarius had earnestly entreated Jesus to come home with him and heal his dying daughter. He knew that if Jesus would just lay His hands on her that she would get well and live. Jesus agreed to come with him, but suddenly there was an interruption. A lady with an issue of blood had pressed through the crowd and touched Him, hoping to be healed. This interruption led to a delay in Jesus getting to Jarius's daughter in time. And, so, she died.

Can you imagine the flood of emotions that must have rushed upon Jarius? I'm sure you can. You know what it is like to get your hopes up and then to have them dashed. Right? I imagine that you have thought the breakthrough is **almost** here. Just as you were getting your spiritual momentum up and going, CRASH! You may think, "If this happens, then ___(Name)___ will be healed, set free, and saved." There is an interruption to your plan – a delay in the progress. Maybe there is even a total halt. It's at times like these that we look for someone to blame. Jarius may have thought: "It is that woman's fault! If she had only not interfered. She blew it for me. Now, there is no use even taking Jesus to see my daughter. It's too late now!" Jarius had received bad news from home – his daughter was dead.

Interruptions and delays are not a problem to Jesus. Bad news or an evil report doesn't hinder Him one bit.

He isn't trapped in time the way we are. He lifts every limit and exceeds every expectation. But, He understands your anxiety and pain. He knows that to you this is taking way too long! And, He knows who you blame and why you blame them. Maybe you think, "If this event hadn't happened to my son/daughter or if he/she would have had a better father or mother, this wouldn't even be happening. If only he/she didn't see so much hypocrisy at church or there would have been a more caring youth pastor…" On and on it goes. The blame game never ends because we desperately are trying to answer the question, "Why?" Maybe, you've decided to answer that question by placing the blame all on yourself. Jesus' priority is not to find out whose fault it is. His desire is to minister to your fear and to get you back on track. You see, the delay has derailed your faith and made you afraid to believe.

Jesus wants to take your hand and start traveling down the road of faith with you. Sweetly, He says, "**Do not be afraid any longer, only keep on believing.**" He doesn't expect you to face the "bad news" by yourself. Together you will walk past all the commotion and weeping.

*"…But putting them all out, He took along the child's father and mother and His own companions, and entered the room **where the child was**"* (Mark 5:40). I imagine that Jarius and his wife thought Jesus was showing respect to visit them and view their daughter's body. Remember, to them, it was too late. Yet, to Jesus, it was just on time for a miracle. Your "too late" is a proving ground for His miracle. He will enter the place where your child is. It doesn't matter to Him if it is your son or daughter's bedroom, a bar, a meth house, a prison cell or a dark alley. Location is not a limit to Him! He will throw out every evil report, every doubt, every obstacle, and every limit. He will shut the devil up! Then, He will give your child back to you.

Prayer:

Lord Jesus, I don't know why You are taking so long to get to my son/daughter. It seems like You may be too late, if I listen to the rumors. But, I am choosing to listen to You and keep on believing. Today, I am giving up trying to figure out whose fault it is. Today, I turn my eyes off of the interruptions, delays, and bad reports. I am taking Your hand. Thank You for walking me through all the commotion. Amen.

Proclamation:

I believe the Lord and I believe His Word. His perfect love drives out all my fear. I refuse to be distracted by bad reports. I believe that Jesus is right on time!

Day 14
New Things

> *Closing yesterday's door opens the door of today's possibilities.*

Isa. 42:9-10 (NKJV) *"Behold the former things have come to pass, new things I declare; before they spring forth I tell you, Sing to the Lord a new song and His praise from the ends of the earth."*

Isa. 43:18-19 (NKJV) *"Do not remember the former things, nor consider the things of old. Behold I will do a new thing, now it shall spring forth; shall you not know it? I will even make a road in the wilderness and rivers in the desert."*

Isa. 48:6-7 (NKJV) *"You have heard; see all this, and will you not declare it? I have made you hear new things from this time, even hidden things, and you did not know them. They are created now and not from the beginning; and before this day you have not heard them..."*

Lam. 3:22-23 (NKJV) *"Through the Lord's mercies we are not consumed, because His compassions fail not. They are new every morning; great is Your faithfulness, 'The Lord is my portion,' says my soul, 'therefore I hope in Him!'"*

Have you ever wished you could start over? If you knew then what you know now... Hindsight really does have 20/20 vision. The word "new" means "not existing before." It refers to the creative power of the Lord to do or make something that has never been done or made in the past. It seems that letting go of the former things – good and bad – dreams and nightmares, wonderful memories and tormenting thoughts, is an integral factor in receiving the new things.

Closing yesterday's door opens
the door of today's possibilities.

I know a lady who kept a baby picture of her 17 year-old on her refrigerator. Longingly, she would look at the picture and wish for those days of innocence when her little girl would give her big hugs and lots of kisses. I was there when the teenager told her mother, "I am not that girl anymore." I could hear in her voice the deep desire to be accepted **now**. She wanted her teenage self to be good enough. That day, I saw

40

a teary mom let go of the previous image and embrace the new. It was necessary.

Sometimes the "road in the wilderness" is still under construction. It may not be a pretty sight. The transition period from caterpillar to butterfly just looks like "bug soup." God wants you to declare the finished product over your offspring. Creation is happening within the cocoon. The choices your son or daughter has made may not have been God's best plan for his/her life; but He is in the transformation business. He is able to "work it together for good" (Rom. 8:28). He can take the trial and the test and turn it into a testimony for His glory.

Have you ever tried singing a new song before the new thing springs forth? Ask the Lord to let you hear heaven's song over your child and then join in. You will experience the awesome, incredible creative power of God. The song may change from day to day based on what He is doing at that time. Sometimes the new song that I sang over my daughters was one I had never heard before – new melody and new lyrics. Other times, it was a familiar song or hymn that was made new to me that day. One day could be "Onward, Christian Soldiers" and the next day could be "I Surrender All."

In your heart, you now begin to close the door on every former thing that has been in your child's life. Now, determine to leave it closed. Do your best to never bring up again the things behind that door. Begin to turn your heart toward the possibilities of the "new thing." Now declare the new thing! Listen for the creative music of heaven and start singing. And remember…one of these days, very soon, the cocoon will crack and the butterfly will appear. You will gasp with astonishment and leap for joy when you see God's new thing.

Prayer:

Lord, please help me to close yesterday's door on all the former things regarding ___(Name's)___ past. Help me, Holy Spirit, and remind me to leave those things behind. Lord, I ask You to let me see and hear the new thing You are doing. I want to sing a new song of hope. Fill my heart with Your new mercies. In Jesus' name, Amen.

New Things

Proclamation:

I declare, in Jesus' name, that ____(Name)____ is going to come into God's new thing for his/her life. I call forth a roadway in his/her wilderness and a river in his/her desert. I proclaim the faithfulness of God and that His new things shall spring forth now. Hallelujah!

Sing a new song!

Day 15
A New Story

A new story has been written in heaven by the finger of God.

John 8: 3-6 *"And the scribes and the Pharisees brought a woman caught in adultery, and having set her in the midst, they said to Him, 'Teacher, this woman has been caught in adultery, in the very act. Now in the Law, Moses commanded us to stone such women; what then shall you say?' And they were saying this, testing Him, in order that they might have grounds for accusing Him. But Jesus stooped down, and with His finger wrote on the ground."*

Col. 2:13b–14 (NKJV) *"He has made us alive together with Him, having forgiven you all trespasses, **having wiped out the handwriting of requirements that was against us,** which was contrary to us. And He has taken it out of the way, having nailed it to the cross."*

Did you ever wonder what Jesus wrote in the dust that day when the religious leaders brought the woman caught in adultery? Perhaps, He wrote a scripture that would bring conviction upon the people of their own sins. Or, maybe He started writing a list of their actual sins. For fear of personal exposure and embarrassment, the accusers would have abandoned their plan to stone the woman. I always wondered how they caught her in "the very act" unless there was a "peeping Tom" in the crowd. And, besides that, where was the man she had been with? Could he be in their midst – one of the leaders? There are lots of unanswered questions in this story.

That's how it is in the life of your son or daughter. So many unexplained circumstances that brought him or her to this point in life. No one **really** knows the truth except Jesus. Everybody has an opinion though. Everyone seems to have an answer to what should happen next. They may even "advise" you as to what the scripture says you, as a parent, should do. It's at these times that "experts" seem to appear. People you may not even normally relate to now may come forward with the rules. Their sentences begin with, "If I were you..."

Just as with the adulterous woman, only one opinion truly matters – His! Why doesn't scripture reveal what He wrote that day? I think it was because He wrote a very personal message to the woman. Symbolically, He wrote in the dust – the place of our beginnings and the place of our endings. The finger that set the world on its axis was writing a new story. He was erasing her history and creating a new beginning. His words are powerful because He is the Word. He cancels out all the *"handwriting of requirements that was against us"* (Col. 2:13b) by the finished work of the cross. Because He went to Calvary and took on the sins and judgments against your child, your precious one is not required to receive what he/she deserves!

I think He may have written in the sand how God saw her and what He said about her. The truth of heaven's decrees cancelled the judgments and religious traditions of men. It is such a relief to know that He has already paid for the punishment that your son/daughter has coming. I can remember times that the enemy would use the scripture to grip my heart with fear. He would say, "Even if she does come back, she will have to pay for what she's done. She will reap what she has sown! It is a spiritual law. There are just natural consequences for such things. God won't break His own law." Then, one day, the Holy Spirit said, "The Father has called for a crop failure on those seeds of rebellion. Their fruit shall not come forth." How I rejoiced! The inevitable "stoning" would not take place. You, too, can rejoice to know that *a new story has been written in heaven by the finger of God.*

And, He has written it on earth in your heart. This story has a happy ending because it agrees with God. Regardless of the opinion, advice, or judgments of others, you must stick to His story. His story erases history and makes all things new.

Prayer:

Lord Jesus, thank You for Calvary. Thank You for erasing ____(Name's)____ sins with Your precious blood. Help me to stick with what You have written in heaven as his/her story. I receive the freedom that comes with Your truth today. Hallelujah!

Proclamation:

In Jesus' name, I enforce on earth the words of heaven over ____(Name)____. I declare that he/she shall fulfill his/her destiny. I bind the judgments of men away from my son/daughter by the blood of Jesus. I proclaim a crop failure on all seeds of rebellion. I say this in agreement with heaven. Amen!

Day 16
An Awakened Ear

> **Running from a BIG calling will require a BIG FISH!**

Isa. 50:4-5 *"...He awakens me morning by morning, He awakens my ear to listen as a disciple. The Lord God has opened my ear; and I was not disobedient, nor did I turn back."*

Jonah 1:17 - 2:1-4 *"And the Lord **appointed** a great fish to swallow Jonah, and Jonah was in the stomach of the fish three days and three nights. **Then** Jonah prayed to the Lord his God from the stomach of the fish, and he said, 'I called out of my distress to the Lord and He answered me. I cried for help from the depth of Sheol, Thou didst hear my voice. For Thou hadst cast me into the deep, into the heart of the seas, and the current engulfed me. All Thy breakers and billows passed over me,' So I said 'I have been expelled from Thy sight. Nevertheless I will look again toward Thy holy temple.'"*

Jonah 2:10 *"Then the Lord commanded the fish, and it vomited Jonah up onto the dry land."*

Jonah 3:1 *"Now the word of the Lord came to Jonah the second time..."*

I am not really sure why our kids think they can run from the purpose and calling of God on their lives. But, I guess all of us try that at least once in some form or fashion. Jonah, like your son or daughter, had a BIG calling on his life. He rebelled because he wanted to do things his way and in his timing. But, also, he ran because he was afraid. Fear can sometimes drive us to run away from God rather than to Him.

It seems that ***running from a BIG calling will require a BIG FISH!***

In the belly of the whale, Jonah decided that God's will for his life was the better choice. There, in the midst of his deep trial, he renewed his vow to God. Disciples are formed in the depths of discipline. It is true anguish to have to see our children swallowed up by troubles and trials and be able to do nothing, isn't it? Yet, we can find comfort in knowing that the "big fish" is "appointed" by God. That means that your child's troubles are custom designed by God. He knows them

45

better than you do and He knows exactly what it will take to bring him/her to their knees. It is in these designed and troubled times that you must be careful not to interfere with the "fish." That fish will become an altar to God in just a little while. I like to call it "the pressure of His presence."

When the whale vomited Jonah onto the dry land, he was not a pretty sight! When your son/daughter comes out of his/her discipline, he/she may not be much for appearances. But, that is the time for lots of grace and mercy. It is, at that time, when God will awaken their ear to hear His voice the "second time." Then, the process of obedience will begin. Step by step your child will walk into the BIG calling. You may from time to time still see some "Pre-Fish" behaviors, but don't let that discourage you. You must remember that **NOW** he/she has an awakened ear and will not turn back. Until then, thank God for the BIG calling and thank God for the BIG FISH!

Prayer:

Lord, today I thank You for Your calling on____(Name)____. I thank You that You have arranged and appointed trials and circumstances to hem him/her in. Please continue to draw him/her to repentance that he/she may call out to You for deliverance and renew his/her commitment to You and Your will. Please help me not to interfere with Your perfect and customized plan. I recognize that You know exactly what it will take and I do not. Thank You for Your unfailing love and mercy. Glorify Your Name!

Proclamation:

____(Name)____, I send the word of repentance and reconciliation into the midst of the depths that you are in. I say to your heart, "Be awakened" and to your ears "Be opened to hear God's voice."

Day 17
Misery Loves Company

Your lonely days are almost over. The King of Kings and Lord of Lords is coming to keep you company.

Hosea 11:8-10 *"'...My heart is turned over within me. All My compassions are kindled. I will not execute My fierce anger; I will not destroy Ephraim again. For I am God and not man, the Holy One in your midst, and I will not come in wrath.' They will walk after the Lord, He will roar like a lion; indeed He will roar, and His sons will come trembling from the west."*

Hosea 14:4 *"'I will heal their backslidings; I will love them freely, for My anger has turned away from them.'"*

Hebrews 4:14-16 *"Since we have a great high priest who has passed through the heavens, Jesus the Son of God, let us hold fast our confession. For we do not have a high priest who cannot sympathize with our weaknesses, but One who has been tempted in all things as we are, yet without sin. Let us draw near with confidence to the throne of grace, that we may receive mercy and may find grace to help in our time of need."*

Loneliness is one of the deepest emotions I can remember. When I thought I had lost my daughter for good, I would feel such deep grief. No one could take her place. I could be surrounded by the rest of the family members and dear friends and yet feel so lonely. The void of the missing one is unexplainable. The amazing thing was that even if she was there – she wasn't. Not the girl I knew. I missed the times that I could freely talk about Jesus and what He was doing without wondering if it would turn her off. I hated that! The egg-shelling that I did so that she would still come around was unbearably uncomfortable. I was trying to hold together some semblance of our relationship. But it was lonely…

In my heart, I would blame her boyfriend or her father. Sometimes, I would blame myself. I would try to act happy and be accepting, but…I was lonely. There were times when our conversation would have awkward moments of silence. Neither of us really knew what to say. And how about the times that I knew she was lying? Those were the

47

worst! Those were the times that she didn't feel safe enough to tell me the truth. I felt such loss that I could literally feel my heart ache in my chest.

Then, one day, He touched me with an awesome revelation. The Lord showed me how His own heart was lonely for her too. He assured me that He was going to pursue her and that I didn't need to. His heart was being pulled by His own desire. I began to realize that I wasn't alone in my loneliness for her. I had company. There is an expression: "Misery loves company." It really is true. I was miserable and the King of the universe came to keep me company. He assured me of His commitment to go after her in hot, passionate pursuit that she would be unable to resist.

But there was one more thing He talked to me about that day...He talked to me about me. He showed me how my all consuming focus on my daughter had left a void in His heart for **me.** He was lonely...for me. I had been focused so much on my own need that many times I had forgotten my fellowship and relationship with Him. I had neglected the One whom I loved the most.

After that, I found that He filled the void and emptiness with more and more of Himself. I loved it and He loved it. Together, we agreed for my daughter – oops, I mean **our** daughter. I still missed her and cried sometimes, but I was not alone.

Today is a day that we are not going to say a special prayer for your son or daughter. Today, we are not going to give you a proclamation to declare. *This time it is about you.* I am going to pray for you, dear friend.

Your lonely days are almost over. The King of Kings and Lord of Lords is coming to keep you company.

Dear Father,

I bring my friend to You today. I especially want to talk to You about the loss and loneliness he/she feels. Lord, I know that You sympathize with our every weakness. Lord, You know exactly how lonely it can be. Would You help my friend to realize that You are lonely too?

Misery Loves Company

Especially, Lord, would You show him/her how much his/her anxious thoughts are taking him/her away from You? Jesus, I know You miss and long for the son or daughter too. But, Lord, I know You miss this one, Your precious child, spending time with You. Today, I ask You to come to the void and empty places of his/her heart and fill them with Your presence. And, Lord, while You are there, I ask You to take the grief and heal the wounds. Holy Spirit, would You give my friend a glimpse of what You are doing with their child? Thank You. In Jesus' name, Amen.

Day 18
Prophesy To The Breath

The words you say are words of life. They are filled and empowered by the Holy Spirit. Your hugs are more than hugs – they are the embrace of His presence and purpose.

Acts 20:9-10 *"And there was a certain young man name Eutychus sitting on the window sill, sinking into a deep sleep, and as Paul kept on talking, he was overcome by sleep, and fell down from the third floor and was picked up dead. But Paul went down and fell upon him and after embracing him, he said, 'Do not be troubled, for his life is in him.'"*

Ezekiel 37:3-5 *"'Son of man, can these bones live?' And I answered, 'O, Lord God, Thou knowest.' Again He said to me, 'Prophesy over these bones and say to them, 'Dry bones, hear the word of the Lord.' Thus says the Lord God to these bones, 'Behold, I will cause breath to enter you and you may come to life.'"*

Ezekiel 37:7, 9 *"So I prophesied as I was commanded; **and as I prophesied,** there was a noise and behold a rattling and the bones came together, bone to its bone...Then He said to me 'Prophesy to the breath, prophesy, son of man...'"*

Hidden in the meaning of Eutychus' name is God's desire and purpose for the young man: "fair, happy, fortunate." Somehow his weariness had overtaken him in the late midnight hour and he had fallen asleep. Normally, falling asleep isn't dangerous. But, on this night, his nap in the third floor window sill cost him his life. Even though he was in the right place at the right time (his window of opportunity), his weary condition caused him to miss his moment to hear the great apostle and he fell.

When we see our kids positioned to receive a great blessing, we get our hopes up that this could be the BIG ANOINTED moment that changes everything. Imagine Eutychus' mother. She may have brought her son to sit at the apostle's feet with hopes that he would be impacted by the inspired teaching. Think how she must have felt when she looked across the crowded room and saw him nodding off. Perhaps, she cleared her throat loudly to get his attention and rouse him. Or maybe she signaled one of the other young people to nudge him. We try this and try that to make sure our kids don't miss out on their window of opportunity – don't we?

I did and said everything I could to give my daughter a wake-up call. I pleaded, prayed, threatened and manipulated—but still she went to sleep. In spite of my carefully devised plans, to make sure she was in the right place at the right time, she still fell. Sometimes, I think she was in so much personal pain that she couldn't bear to stay awake. When she fell, I thought for sure that she was dead. I saw no signs of life.

Maybe you have had to watch your son or daughter tumble headlong into the darkness. You wonder how he/she could have missed such an obvious opportunity for a better life. But, long before the fall was the sleep. You saw the fall coming, didn't you? You tried to stop it. Yet the sleep the enemy had lulled him/her into was too deep.

The miraculous life-giving embrace of Paul revived Eutychus. I suppose that hug was packed full of the Holy Spirit's power! Paul had bravely prophesied over his dead body, *"Do not be afraid, his life is in him."* From that day on, I doubt if the young man ever again missed his window of opportunity.

Just like Paul, *the words you say are words of life. They are filled and empowered by the Holy Spirit. Your hugs are more than hugs – they are the embrace of His presence and purpose.*

A hug doesn't mean that you approve and agree with everything your son or daughter is doing. A hug is a secret weapon of impartation! If your child will not allow you to embrace him/her or is out of your reach completely, ask God to send a Paul into his/her life to represent God and to represent you.

Prayer:

Lord, I release all of my attempts to wake up ___(Name)___. I want to minister Your way to my child. Please show me my windows of opportunity. Live and love through me. Lord, if it's not my words or hugs that will revive him/her, please send somebody. In Jesus' name, Amen.

Prophesy To The Breath

Proclamation:

Today, I will not fear but I speak forth the word of life over
___(Name)___. I say, "Your life is in you!" I prophesy to the breath
and say, "Breathe upon my child!" I proclaim, "You shall live and not
die and you shall declare the goodness and glory of God!" Hallelujah!

Day 19
Help From Heaven

God has "Good Samaritans" already traveling on your son's or daughter's road.

Luke 10:30, 33-34 *"Jesus replied and said, 'A certain man was going down from Jerusalem to Jericho; and he fell among robbers and they stripped him and beat him and went off leaving him half dead...But a certain Samaritan, who was upon a journey, came upon him; and when he saw him, he felt compassion, and came to him, and bandaged up his wounds, pouring oil and wine on them; and he put him on his own beast, and brought him to an inn, and took care of him.'"*

It was a friend who lived in another state who first alerted me to the danger my daughter was in. I thought the young man she was dating was "godly and a gentleman." I had even been impressed with his manners. He would say, "Yes ma'am" and "No ma'am." He would stand if a lady entered the room and would open the car door for my daughter. I was swept off my feet right into blindness and deception. When my praying friend called she said, "She is in danger. Whoever she is dating is involved in witchcraft!" I didn't know whether to be angry or afraid. My pride was hurt too. "Could this be going on under my nose and I missed it? How could I be so deceived?" The thoughts just raced through my head. I felt really disqualified as a minister. I thought, "If I can't even discern what's going on with my own daughter, what right have I got to tell anyone else anything?"

Finally, I went to my daughter with the information that the Lord had given my friend. Of course, she was defensive and denied it. She was "in love" and very offended about the accusations against her boyfriend. Her defensiveness was my clue that something truly was in darkness. I began to pray with a few of my close prayer partners that the deception would be broken and that she would see the truth for herself. It was only a few weeks before our prayers were answered. She realized what she was in and wanted to get out of it. However, she was very afraid of her boyfriend. It was at this time she told us that he was part of a gang and that he carried a gun. He had a very "dark side" that she had kept hidden.

Her sister was away at college and she proved to be the Good Samaritan.

Help From Heaven

She coached her younger sister through the break up and then invited her to California to get away from a very dangerous situation. The boyfriend didn't give up easily and even began to stalk her. So, we sent her away to YWAM (Youth With A Mission) where she could receive some ministry and also be far away from him.

God sent help from heaven. I thank God for my friend who called and alerted me, for my oldest daughter's help and wisdom, for my prayer partners and for YWAM. My daughter had been taken off the course of her journey and had been "beaten" and "left by the side of the road by robbers" and I never knew it. However, sometimes, I was like the priest and Levite who passed on the other side of the road. I was so "busy" with the ministry that I couldn't see my wounded daughter in the ditch. Part of me really didn't **want** to see because her condition was a reflection of me and my failures. I know the Lord had tried to give me hints before my friend called but I just ignored the warning signs. I don't know all the reasons why I did that. Mostly, it was my spiritual pride. Pride is blinding and deceptive. I repented to my daughter and I repented to God.

The Lord is merciful and faithful to His Word. In spite of my failures, He sent "Good Samaritans" to my daughter who carried her into a place of healing and safety. It's hard sometimes to look back and realize that I didn't have the oil and wine that she needed – but it's wonderful to know He had His friends who stepped into the gap. However, there have been plenty of times since then, on the path of life, that God has used me to minister to her.

Today, the Lord wants to minister to your regrets: the ones that have to do with your missed moments of opportunity. If you simply repent, He promises to heal you and your land, which is your inheritance (see 2 Chron. 7:14). He wants you to know that your child's deliverance and healing do not depend on you.

God has "Good Samaritans" already traveling on your son's or daughter's road.

He has special friends of His who will pour in oil and wine and who will aid in bringing them to their destination. And when they arrive…you will be waiting with open arms.

Help From Heaven

Prayer:

Lord, I pray that You will open my eyes to any places that I am in denial or deception about my children. Show me the truth so that I can pray and minister effectively. I repent of spiritual pride. Lord, I recognize that I don't have all the answers and ministry that they need. Please send "Good Samaritans" into their lives to minister to them. Dear God, prepare me to receive them when they return. Thank You for the help You are sending. In Jesus' name, Amen.

Day 20
A Dream Come True

> *The Lord can see what you cannot see. He can see that the enemy's days are numbered and He laughs.*

Ps. 126:1-3 *"When the Lord brought back the captive ones in Zion, we were like those who dream. Then our mouth was filled with laughter, and our tongue with joyful shouting; then they said among the nations, 'The Lord has done great things for them! The Lord has done great things for us. We are glad.'"*

Ps. 16:11 *"Thou wilt make known to me the path of life, in Thy presence is fullness of joy; in Thy right hand there are pleasures forever."*

Ps. 37:12-13 *"The wicked plots against the righteous, and gnashes at him with his teeth. The Lord laughs at him; for He sees his day is coming."*

Ps. 30:5 *"...Weeping may last for the night, but a shout of joy comes in the morning."*

Can you imagine the joy you will feel the day your precious one comes back to the Lord? You will feel like you are dreaming. You have gotten so used to the nightmare of their captivity that you will hardly believe it. You won't know whether to laugh or cry. Probably, you will do some of both. It will seem like a flash flood of emotions. You may feel like saying, "Somebody pinch me," just so you can be sure you really are awake and that it really is happening. It truly will be a *"joy inexpressible and full of glory!"* (1 Pet. 1:8).

I remember, in the midst of the darkest days, that I heard the strangest sound. I heard the sound of rejoicing. The Lord was laughing! I thought I must finally be going crazy. "Why is He laughing? Can't He see my tear-soaked pillow? Maybe He hasn't noticed that things aren't looking so good." It was a laugh like I had never heard. It wasn't a giggle. It wasn't a belly laugh. It was like thunder that predicted the coming rain. It was all-knowing and creative. Suddenly, I knew it was mocking His enemy and it was rejoicing in His triumph. Only God can laugh like that!

56

A Dream Come True

*The Lord can see what you cannot see. He can see
that the enemy's days are numbered and He laughs.*

That sound changed my whole outlook. I purposed in my heart to join heaven's rejoicing and praise Him for the return of my daughter. The sound of my prayers turned from mourning over the trials to joy over His triumph. I knew that the devil was confused by my new found joy. That day, I decided to live in my dream come true instead of the nightmare. The only way that was possible was to live in His presence rather than in my problems.

Sometimes, for no apparent reason, I could feel His joy begin to bubble up in me. I knew that was the sound of His victory – it was the sound of my dream come true. God was laughing at His enemy and that made me smile.

Today would be a good day to confuse your enemy with joy. Go ahead and praise the Lord with rejoicing. Your dream is coming true and it begins right now, right here with you! God says, "Go ahead and laugh! Look and see! Your enemy's day is coming!"

Prayer:

Lord, thank You that my dream is coming true. Help me to hear the sound of Your rejoicing and to join with You to celebrate the devil's defeat. I want to live in Your presence and experience Your true joy. Instead of sorrow and heaviness, I want to wear the garment of praise. Be glorified in my praises! Amen.

Proclamation:

I rejoice in You. I praise You for my child's freedom from captivity. I thank You for making my dreams come true! Hallelujah! The joy of the Lord is increasing in me and I have strength. I say to the forces of darkness: "Your day is coming! My God laughs at you and so do I!"

Day 21
Happy Holidays

God's signals to us are often times a little insignificant something that we could miss if we aren't looking for it.

Luke 2:10-12 *"And the angel said to them, 'Do not be afraid, for behold I bring you good news of a great joy which shall be for all the people; for today in the city of David there has been born for you a Savior, who is Christ the Lord. And this will be **a sign to you:** you will find a baby wrapped in cloths, and lying in a manger.'"*

Luke 2:14 *"'Peace on earth! Good will toward men!'"*

Ps. 86:16-17 *"Turn to me and be gracious to me; oh grant Thy strength to Thy servant, and save the son of Thy handmaid. **Show me a sign for good,** that those who hate me may see it, and be ashamed, because Thou, O Lord, has helped me and comforted me."*

Holidays are sometimes the hardest times of the year. These are days that are supposed to be joyful. These are days when we gather as a family to celebrate, give gifts, eat yummy food and love each other. Our family traditions give us a sense of security and predictability. There is even a strange comfort in the various dysfunctions and idiosyncrasies of our family members. Probably, because we can count on the sameness, we feel oddly stable. As our kids grow up, we pass on our traditions and recipes, not only recipes for special desserts – but recipes for living. Our hearts rejoice as we see them as children open presents with glee and taste our holiday cooking. But, even more joyful are the times when we see them pick up the torch and the family legacy to make it their own.

So, when one of our children is not right with God, our holiday world is shaken to the core. If our backslidden one chooses not to participate in our family gathering, it feels like such a deep rejection. More than on regular days, right? Of course, there are the holidays when he/she is present but is making it clear that they don't really want to be there. Or, just because of the signs of the world on them, you know that he/she is not choosing to live for Jesus. On holidays, it glares…it's in your face…you can't ignore it!

Happy Holidays!

Suppose you are the one invited to the wayward one's home to celebrate Christmas. You enter the house that seems to be void of any sign of the Christ. Everything seems so out of sync. This isn't how you taught them. You wander around wondering where in the room to sit or what to do or say. You try busying yourself with some kitchen chores or staring at the television. You wonder if it will ever end. That night when you fall into bed, you are not having visions of sugar plums! You are begging God to change things before next year.

When the angels appeared to the shepherds in the field outside of Bethlehem, they announced the good news of peace to all men. They declared, "A Savior is born." The sign of the long awaited Messiah and King would be a baby in a humble stable.

God's signals to us are often times a little insignificant something that we could miss if we aren't looking for it.

After hearing such a flashy announcement, I wonder if it seemed a little anti-climatic to stare into the face of a baby in a manger. Yet, God said, this would be the sign of His coming kingdom and glory. Wrapped in swaddling cloths was God's mystery.

The next time you have a holiday gathering consider looking for a sign from God. He wants to show you a sign for good to give you hope for the days ahead. I remember seeing a tiny tear in my daughter's eye when her children sang "Happy Birthday" to Jesus. That tear was all I needed. It was as if God secretly winked at me and smiled. At that moment, I didn't really need the security of the traditions I had treasured. The sentimentalism of the past seasons did not tug at my heart anymore that day. I had seen a glimpse of the future and I had hope.

Prayer:

Lord, please prepare me for the holidays. Help me to see what You are doing; show me a sign for good. Lord, I let go of what I think our family celebration should be like. Do a new thing in our family and invade our traditions with Your ways and presence. In Jesus' name, Amen.

Happy Holidays!

Proclamation:

I speak to the blinders of tradition and sentimentalism and say, "Be gone from my eyes!" I declare that this year I will see God's sign for good in my children and family! I release the words of "peace" and "good will" to our holidays.

Day 22
Peace, Be Still!

He's in your boat and He has the word you need to calm the storm.

Phil. 4:7-8 *"And the peace of God, which surpasses all comprehension, shall guard your hearts and your minds in Christ Jesus. Finally, brethren, whatever is true, whatever is honorable, whatever is right, whatever is pure, whatever is lovely, whatever is of good repute, if there is any excellence and if anything worthy of praise, let your mind dwell on these things. The things you have learned and received and heard and seen in me practice these things; and the God of peace shall be with you."*

Mark 4:38-39 *"And He Himself was in the stern, asleep on the cushion; and they awoke Him and said to Him, 'Teacher, do you not care that we are perishing?' And being aroused, He rebuked the wind and said to the sea, 'Peace, be still' and the wind died down and it became perfectly calm."*

Rom. 16:20 *"And the God of peace will soon crush Satan under your feet. The grace of our Lord Jesus be with you."*

Peace defined: "a state of mutual harmony between people or groups; cessation of or freedom from any strife or dissension; freedom of the mind from annoyance, distraction, anxiety, an obsession, etc.; a state of tranquility or serenity." (Dictionary.com)

The worst storms are the unpredicted ones: the ones that kick up on a clear day when there is no time to protect ourselves. Just when you think that everything is secure and stable (at least for the time being), the boat begins to rock. You are in the middle of the sea and start rowing furiously to get to the other side before it is a full-blown hurricane. You've been here before – when the winds suddenly shift. The phone call that broke your heart. The night you waited and waited for your child to come home. The shouting match that you wished you had not participated in. The "secrets" you found in their bedroom. The whirlwind is indescribable. It sets off a whole chain of events that begins first in your mind. The panic in your chest lets you know that the battle has begun **again.** There may have been a short reprieve from crisis, but now, here it is again. The huge waves won't let you go into denial and pretend the storm isn't there.

Peace, Be Still!

You have to do something! So, you try doing the only thing you know how to do: Grab the oars and start rowing! Your efforts are fruitless...and suddenly you remember: Jesus is in the boat! "Why is He sleeping? How can He relax with all that is going on? Doesn't He care?" The thoughts pound against your mind like the waves of the sea. He must know something that you don't, if He can be in such peace in the face of such obvious danger. The destructive behaviors and backslidings of your son or daughter have not thrown Him into a panic.

And, so, you call out to Him for help. With a word, He speaks to the storm and quiets the waves. If you would have known that was all it took, you wouldn't have wasted all the time and effort in rowing. May I tell you a secret? Truly, the storm is not what your son or daughter is doing. The storm is your reaction to what he/she is doing. The storm is in your mind. After all, it is your boat.

Sometimes in the midst of the noise of our own thoughts, we forget Who lives in us. We try to deal with the turmoil of our emotions the best way we can. I don't know what you do to gain peace of mind. I used all kinds of "oars:" food, television, calling my friend, sleep, shopping, exercise, and general busyness. At the most, these gave me minimum relief.

Finally, I remembered that Jesus was in my boat quietly waiting. When I turned my attention from the waves onto Him, Jesus, inside of me, woke up! The One Who is the Word spoke through me, "Peace, be still! Be still and know I am God." As quickly as the storm had come, it was gone. My mind became at rest; my body relaxed; and I found myself on "the other side." Once Jesus had control of the boat, the disciples reached their destination without rowing. I have found that my greatest efforts are useless without His Word and His presence. There is no peace in just trying to manage the storm of my mind with superficial, temporary means. Do you need peace of mind today? Are you tired of rowing? Why not wake up Jesus?

He's in your boat and He has the word
you need to calm the storm.

Peace, Be Still!

Regardless of what your son or daughter is doing today, you can have the peace that passes understanding.

Prayer:

Lord, Jesus, I need Your peace today. I am weary and tired of "rowing." I am frustrated with my fruitless efforts. I turn my mind and thoughts away from the storm to look to You. Please forgive me for trying to gain peace my own way. Will you arise in me and fill my mouth with Your word? Thank You for bringing me to the "other side." In Your Name, Amen.

Proclamation:

Today, I speak to the storm of anxious thoughts in my mind, and I say to you, "Peace, be still!" I have the mind of Christ and His peace crushes Satan under my feet. Hallelujah for His victory in me!

Day 23
A Day To Wait On The Lord

Today is a day set aside for waiting on the Lord and receiving new strength. As you wait before Him, reflect on all He has brought you through. Allow Him to give you a fresh look and new perspective of the future. Let the wind of His Spirit blow over you, refresh you and give you new life.

Isa. 40:28-31 *"Do you not know? Have you not heard? The Everlasting God, the Lord, the Creator of the ends of the earth does not become weary or tired. His understanding is inscrutable. He gives strength to the weary, and to him who lacks might He increases power. Though youths grow weary and tired, and vigorous young men stumble badly, yet those who wait for the Lord will gain new strength; they will mount up with wings like eagles, they will run and not get tired, they will walk and not become weary."*

Ps. 25:4-6 *"Make me know Thy ways, O Lord; teach me Thy paths. Lead me in Thy truth and teach me, for Thou art the God of my salvation; for Thee I will wait all the day. Remember, O Lord, Thy compassion and Thy lovingkindnesses, for they have been from of old."*

Ps. 27:13-14 *"I would have despaired unless I had believed that I would see the goodness of the Lord in the land of the living. Wait for the Lord; be strong, and let your heart take courage; yes, wait for the Lord."*

Ps. 46:10-11 *"'Cease striving and know that I am God, I will be exalted among the nations, I will be exalted in the earth.' The Lord of hosts is with us; the God of Jacob is our stronghold."*

Ps. 62:5-6 *"My soul, wait in silence for God only, for my hope is from Him. He only is my rock and my salvation, my stronghold; I shall not be shaken."*

Ps. 23:1-3 *"The Lord is my shepherd, I shall not want. He makes me lie down in green pastures; He leads me beside quiet waters. He restores my soul; He guides me in the paths of righteousness for His name's sake."*

Ps. 37:34 *"Wait for the Lord, and keep His way, and He will exalt you to inherit the land; when the wicked are cut off, you will see it."*

Day 24
The Look Of Love

> **In spite of the denials of darkness, the morning is coming.**

Ps. 41:9 *"Even my close friend, in whom I trusted, who ate my bread, has lifted up his heel against me."*

Ps. 55:12-13 *"For it is not an enemy who reproaches me, then I could bear it; nor is it one who hates me who has exalted himself against me, then I could hide myself from him. But it is you, a man, my equal, my companion and my familiar friend. We who had sweet fellowship together, walked in the house of God in the throng."*

Matt. 26:74-75 *"Then he began to curse and swear, 'I do not know the man!' And immediately a cock crowed. And Peter remembered the word which Jesus had said, 'Before a cock crows, you will deny Me three times.' And he went out and wept bitterly."*

Luke 22:61 *"And the Lord turned and looked at Peter. And Peter remembered the word of the Lord…"*

It is not only the denying of the Lord that hurts, but it also is the denying of you. When he/she left Him, you were left too. This one who looks so much like you now has very few resemblances to you. He/she may have your eyes or your curly hair, but he/she no longer has your heart for Jesus. The denial feels so much like a betrayal – a breaking of a covenant alliance. It's the kind of thing you would expect from your worst enemy – not your flesh and blood. It feels like everything you are and have stood for is being treated like rubbish. They may act like the things you have always said and taught are ridiculous. When you speak, they look at you like you are speaking a foreign language – as though you are from another planet.

Sometimes, I would wonder if I was an embarrassment to my daughter. Did she keep her distance because her friends would think I was weird? It really hurt that she did not want to be identified with me. Well-meaning friends would try to console me by saying that it was the Lord who was in me that she was rejecting. They would say that it really wasn't me being rejected, and so I shouldn't take it so personally. I couldn't help it. It felt so personal!

The Look Of Love

As Peter stood warming himself by the fire, Jesus was standing before the religious leaders being interrogated. False witnesses were testifying against Him. Peter kept a safe distance and took care of his own needs. However, he was curious and he cared about what would happen to Jesus. After all, he had cut off the soldier's ear in the garden. No one should wonder about his commitment! Peter's instincts had caused him to grab the sword in the heat of the moment. Yet, when a slave girl asked him if he knew the Lord, he cursed and denied Him. Only Jesus knew that the intensity of that night's pressure would reveal the weakness of his character. It wasn't that the slave girl was more intimidating than the soldier in the garden. Her question was the final straw that tipped the balances of his heart. It had pressed Peter to choose between identifying with Jesus unreservedly or to deny Him. After Peter denied Him three times, the rooster crowed.

I don't know what pressures of life caused your child to turn and go the way of the world. It may have been peer pressure, relational disappointments, or church people's hypocrisy. Whatever it was revealed what was already there: carnal nature. The flesh which opposes the ways of God was uncovered and wrong choices were made. Instead of repentance there was pride, rebellion, and denial.

I think, when the rooster crowed, the barrier in Peter's heart was split and the Holy Spirit rushed in upon the Lord's words. Jesus turned and looked at him. In that instant, Peter remembered His words and wept. A new day dawned. Just a few weeks later, he boldly preached the message of the gospel on Pentecost. I encourage you to consider that:

In spite of the denials of darkness, the morning is coming.

The sound of the rooster awakened Peter's soul to remember the look of love, and he was convicted of his sin. Your child will be somewhere minding his own business and something will be a startling reminder of the word of the Lord. Suddenly, he/she will realize Jesus is lovingly and longingly looking at him/her. Your son/daughter will repent and a new day will dawn.

The Look Of Love

Prayer:

Lord, please heal my heart of the rejections and denials of
___(Name)___. The distance between us is such a big gulf. Sometimes,
I think it is too much of a breach to ever be healed. Please, come and
be the repairer of the breach. How we need You, Lord! Would You
awaken my child's soul and remind him/her of Your word? Surround
him/her with Your love today. I know it will be impossible to resist!
In Your Wonderful Name, Amen.

Proclamation:

___(Name)___, I speak to you to hear, remember and recognize the
word and calling of the Lord. I break the power of betrayal from our
relationship by the reconciliatory power of the Blood! I call you to
return to the Lord and to your calling, in Jesus' name.

Day 25
A Fresh Anointing

> When the anointing rises within you, you become aware of The Greater One.

Isa. 61:1-2 *"The Spirit of the Lord is upon me because the Lord has anointed me to bring good news to the afflicted; He has sent me to bind up the broken hearted, to proclaim liberty to captives, and freedom to prisoners; to proclaim the favorable year of the Lord and the day of vengeance of our God..."*

Isa. 59:21 *"'And as for Me, this is My covenant with them,' declares the Lord: 'My Spirit which is upon you, and My words which I have put in your mouth, shall not depart from your mouth, nor from the mouth of your offspring, nor from the mouth of your offspring's offspring,' says the Lord, 'from now and forever.'"*

Ps. 92:10-11 *"...I have been anointed with fresh oil, and my eye has looked exultantly upon my foes..."*

Isa. 10:27 *"So it will be in that day, that his burden will be removed from your shoulders and his yoke from your neck, and the yoke will be broken because of the anointing."*

Today, the Holy Spirit wants to pour out His anointing and glory upon you in a new way. You need the anointing to break the bondages of oppression and depression. You need the anointing to cause His word to come alive in your heart. Without the anointing, our times with God can be stale and our Bible reading will be just words on a page. The anointing will lift you out of the circumstances and into His throne room. From there, you gain His perspective and new strength.

When the anointing rises within you, you become aware of The Greater One.

His authority and power will give you a confidence and boldness to take your stand against the devil. It breaks the power of his accusations and condemnations. The anointing will give you a new look at Calvary and the power of the cross. The anointing will give you a new garment and a new look. Your suppressed identity will begin to emerge and the grave clothes of this last season will fall from you. The anointing will cause you to bless the Lord and will fill your mouth with His praises.

A Fresh Anointing

You will begin to sing a new song with gratitude for the breakthrough. You will begin to have your faith arise and declare His covenant over you and your descendants. Nothing will be impossible to you! The anointing will break you out of unbelief's prison. The anointing will tell you the truth and the truth will set you free!

Receive a fresh anointing!

Prayer:

Lord, I thank You for Your Holy Spirit who fills me and anoints me with fresh oil. Please remove my old garments of grief, depression, and oppression. Set me free from the prison of unbelief. Increase my faith and cause me to stand with authority in the covenant blessing. I receive the new anointing, right now. Hallelujah!

Proclamation:

In Jesus' name and because of my covenant with Him, I declare that His word will not depart from my mouth or from the mouth of my offspring nor from the mouth of my offspring's offspring. The Holy Spirit shall be upon me and upon them and He will not depart from us! I enforce Calvary's victory over me and my family by the blood of Jesus. Amen and Amen!

Day 26
Free To Be Me

Isa. 54:13, 17 *"'And all your sons* (and daughters) *shall be taught of the Lord and the well being of your sons* (and daughters) *will be great... No weapon formed against you will prosper and every tongue that accuses you in judgment, you will condemn. This is the heritage of the servants of the Lord, and their vindication is from Me,' declares the Lord."*

John 11:44 *"He who had died came forth, bound hand and foot with wrappings, and his face was wrapped around with a cloth. Jesus said to them, 'Unbind him, and let him go.'"*

Matt. 18:18 *"'Truly I say to you, whatever you shall bind on earth shall be bound in heaven, and whatever you loose on earth shall be loosed in heaven.'"*

When the Lord stood before the tomb, He commanded that the stone be removed. The dead man's sister reminded Jesus that her brother, Lazarus, had been dead for four days and that by now *"he stinketh."* Upon Jesus' insistence, the stone was removed and the dead man was raised – even though he smelled like a deteriorating corpse. Aren't you glad that Jesus is not limited by our understanding?

The now alive Lazarus still looked like and smelled like a dead man. The wrappings of the grave still confined him. His feet (that which would walk him into his next season) and his hands (that which would give him the ability to take hold of his future) were bound. His face (that which distinguished him and gave him his unique identity) was covered. Jesus commanded those who had bound him to loose him.

As our children begin to come forth, it will be up to us to make sure the wrappings are removed. We may discover that we, ourselves, have gotten tied up in the death identity. We may not know what to do to get free ourselves and to then set them free. The judgments that people may have made on us regarding our children's conditions can become a weapon in the enemy's hand to keep us in captivity and condemnation. Possibly, you may have actually agreed with the judgments that have been levied against you and your children. I know that I did. I discovered that there was an ungodly power in that agreement.

Free To Be Me

I believed the lies about my failures. The devil had formed the judgments into a very powerful weapon that literally bound me and kept me from exercising my God-given authority.

I finally realized that by being in personal bondage to these judgments, I could not loose my children from their captivity. Part of my captivity was based in my own pride. I had to admit that I was personally embarrassed and took responsibility for my daughter's decisions. It made me look bad! (Just as Martha had said, *"Lord, by now he stinks."*) That pride was the stone that had to be removed by deep repentance. With humility comes a new measure of authority and freedom. I realized that *the first person who had to be free was ....me!*

Once I had repented, I then could begin to rise up and condemn the judgments, removing their power as a weapon against me and my children

When your children begin the process of freedom, you will play a vital role in removing the wrappings (judgments). You must realize that you have the authority to loose them and let them go. As you begin to unwrap your son or daughter, you will see their hidden identity and purpose begin to be revealed. Before you know it, he/she will be walking and talking like Jesus. The stench of the former things will be gone! You will both be free!

Prayer:

Father, please forgive me for any place I have agreed with the judgments against myself or my children. Please forgive me for my foolish pride. Set me free so that I can agree with You and take my authority on behalf of my children. Please release me from the grave clothes of judgments that have bound me. In Jesus' name, Amen.

Proclamation:

Every judgment against ____(Name)____, I rise up and condemn. I break the power of any agreement with those judgments by the authority of the name and blood of Jesus. I say to ____(Name)____, "I loose and unbind you, and let you go free!" I say to the devil, "These weapons will no longer prosper!"

Day 27
Let There Be Light!

In the deepest dungeon of sin, He will be waiting... waiting on the Word – "Let there be light!"

Ps. 139:1-5 *"O Lord, Thou has searched me and known me. Thou dost know when I sit down and rise up. Thou dost understand my thought from afar. Thou dost scrutinize my path and my lying down, and art intimately acquainted with all my way. Even before there is a word on my tongue, behold, O Lord, Thou dost know it all. Thou hast enclosed me behind and before, and laid Thy hand upon me."*

Ps. 139:7 *"Where can I go from Thy Spirit? Or where can I flee from Thy presence?"*

Ps. 139:16 *"Thine eyes have seen my unformed substance; and in Thy book they were all written, the days that were ordained for me, when as yet there was not one of them."*

Gen. 1:2-3 *"And the earth was formless and void, and darkness was over the surface of the deep; and the Spirit of God was moving over the surface of the waters. Then God said, 'Let there be light' and there was light."*

Before your child was born, God ordained every single day of his/her life. The Spirit of God hovered over his/her unformed substance just as He had moved over the formless void places of the earth before creation. It's amazing to think that the same Spirit who fulfilled the Word of God to create the universe brooded over your baby in the womb. When my daughter was wandering in darkness, I found comfort in the knowledge that He was able to overtake that empty, void place with His marvelous light.

Isn't it awesome to think that no matter where your son or daughter goes, the Holy Spirit will be there to meet him/her? Before he/she can even think of getting out of bed in the morning or lying down at night, He is there.

In the deepest dungeon of sin, He will be waiting... waiting on the Word – *"Let there be light!"*

Let There Be Light!

When you are wondering what your kids are doing or where they may be, He knows and is there. He knows their plans before they do and He knows them better than you ever will.

So, why do we worry? Why do our hearts pound with fear? If He is there, isn't He watching and waiting to deliver them? I asked myself these questions. Quietly, He spoke upon my heart, "You don't **really believe** that I am there. You don't **really believe** that her days are numbered and written in the book of heaven. You believe the world's philosophy that she is in charge of her own destiny. Nothing could be further from the truth! Did you dedicate her to Me when she was a baby? Then, she is Mine."

Maybe, you need to repent like I did that day. I still have to repent of my unbelief from time to time regarding my kids. The fear isn't completely conquered yet. But, the more I get to know Him and experience His love, the more I am convinced of His keeping power. Consider the truth that He has enclosed and hemmed your child in with the fence of His love. It is a strong fence…stronger than you will ever be. Why not decide to believe Him and His word today? Try to leave them completely under His shadow of brooding. Creative miracles happen in that place! When the light comes, the voids will be filled and the darkness will flee.

Prayer:

Today, Lord, I repent for my fears and unbelief. Help me to trust Your Holy Spirit to hover over____(Name)____ and to be wherever he/she is. I want to know You more so that I can experience more of Your perfect love. Thank You for the power of Your love that pursues and protects my children. In Jesus' name, Amen.

Proclamation:

Today, I agree with the Word of God and I speak His word into the dark void places of ____(Name's)____ life. I say to the darkness, "Let there be light!" And to the meaningless empty places, I say, "Be filled with the Holy Spirit." Hallelujah!

Day 28
A Day To Trust

Leaning on God is the best thing to do when you feel like you don't know what to do. One time I was crying to the Lord about my daughter and I heard myself saying, "I love You, but I don't trust You." The Holy Spirit taught me, that day, that trust is even deeper than faith in my relationship with God. He explained that faith is based on His word and trust is based upon His character and nature. This is the example He gave me: "If your friend told you that he had mailed you a check, and the check didn't arrive – even though he had given his word – what would you do?" I said, "I would know that something had happened to the mail – maybe it was sent to the wrong address or lost." He said, "Because you **know** your friend is a man of his word and you know he has integrity, you would **trust** him. You would call him and let him know that something or someone had hindered you from receiving what he had sent. You would never question if he had sent it because you **know** him."

Likewise, if you trust the Lord, and you have not received the promise He has sent you, you do not doubt Him because you **know** Him and His character of integrity. If you find yourself questioning or blaming Him, you will know that is an area in your heart that you do not know Him yet. Now, when I realize that I don't trust Him in an area (especially with my kids), I ask Him to reveal Himself to me and help me to get to know Him better. It may be that I need to know Him as Provider, or Healer, or Restorer, or Deliverer. Maybe I need to know Him more as Father, Friend, or Husband.

Today, let Him reveal Himself to you in new ways and let Him show you in what areas you need to know Him and trust Him.

Ps. 37:3-6 *"Trust in the Lord, and do good; dwell in the land and cultivate faithfulness. Delight yourself in the Lord; and He will give you the desires of your heart. Commit your way to the Lord, trust also in Him, and He will do it. And He will bring forth your righteousness as the light and your judgment as the noonday."*

Ps. 62:8 *"Trust in Him at all times, O people; pour out your heart before Him; God is a refuge for us."*

A Day To Trust

Prov. 3:5-8 *"Trust in the Lord with all your heart, and do not lean on your own understanding. In all your ways acknowledge Him, and He will make your paths straight. Do not be wise in your own eyes; fear the Lord and turn away from evil. It will be healing to your body, and refreshment to your bones."*

Day 29
Pursue And Recover All

> *Strengthen yourself in God and then...* *"Pursue, for you shall surely overtake them, and you shall surely recover all."*

1 Sam. 30:3-4, 6 *"And when David and his men came to the city, behold it was burned with fire; and their wives and their sons and their daughters had been taken captive.* **Then David and the people who were with him lifted their voices and wept until there was no strength in them to weep**...*Moreover David was greatly distressed because the people spoke of stoning him, for all the people were embittered, each one because of his sons and daughters. But* **David strengthened himself in the Lord his God.**"

1 Sam. 30:18a *"So David recovered all that the Amalekites had taken..."*

When David and his men returned from battle, they discovered that their city had been burned down and their wives and children had been carried away by the enemy. David and the people cried and cried until they couldn't cry anymore. Has that ever happened to you? When you cried until you collapsed from exhaustion, you may have wondered if you would live through the whole ordeal. That is the time when you need your spouse, other family members and friends to rise to the occasion and support you. You need a strong arm to lean on. But, for reasons of their own, they can't do that for you. They have their own problems and pain. That is what happened to David. His team shared the same grief and loss. They couldn't help him and they couldn't help themselves. Not only that: In their weakened state, they turned on David and wanted to kill him.

If your spouse and/or friends are hurting as much as you are, they may not be able to support and encourage you. And, you may not be able to support them either. Otherwise unified marriages and relationships can begin to disintegrate under the fiery pressure of losing our children. This is where the "blame game" usually begins. It is at this time you may find yourselves projecting your pain onto the other person and you each begin to blame the other for the condition of your child. If the "blame game" continues, your lifetime best friend can become your dreaded enemy. This is the devil's strategy: Divide and conquer!

You, like David, will be at a crossroads. You will have to make a critical choice. Will you dive into the pit of self-pity and victimization or will you strengthen yourself in the Lord? In your exhausted state, you must make the conscious decision to get up and bless the Lord. *"Bless the Lord, oh my soul"* (Ps. 103:1), David cried out. He spoke to his own emotions to line up with God's mind and will. As his soul was restored in the presence of God, his body was strengthened for the fight. David's new-found strength must have been contagious because 400 men arose to pursue the enemy with him! (I think part of his new strength must have come as he forgave his friends who had blamed him. If he hadn't forgiven them, he could not have fought the battle along side them.) David and his men recovered their children and wives as well as all the plunder that had been stolen.

I don't know if your spouse and/or friends will stop blaming and begin strengthening themselves in the Lord. Whether they choose to do that or not, you can choose to stop wasting time and energy on the "blame game." You can stop blaming, forgive those who blame you, and strengthen yourself in the Lord. Praise is powerful! When you praise, you will find yourself in the presence of the Lord and will gain new strength to pursue and recover your children. It is possible that your new approach to the problem could be contagious.

Don't settle for anything less than a full recovery of your children. The enemy stole them and carried them away and he has to give them back! He also has to give back the plunder: lost time, loss of relationship, loss of money, loss of identity and calling. *"But when he (the thief) is found, he must repay sevenfold, he must give all the substance of his house"* (Prov. 6:31).

Today's word to you is:

Strengthen yourself in God and then…"Pursue, for you shall surely overtake them, and you shall surely recover all."
(1 Sam. 30:8)

Pursue And Recover All

Prayer:

Lord, please forgive me for anytime I have blamed others for my child's condition. Lord, I forgive those who have blamed or judged me. Right now, I will bless and praise You! Please meet me in my praises and grant me new strength. In Jesus' name, Amen.

Proclamation:

"Bless the Lord, O my soul, and let everything within me bless His name. Bless the Lord, O my soul and forget none of His benefits!" (Ps. 103:1-2)

I receive the strength of the Lord and I say to the enemy: "You have been found out and you must repay. I demand the return of ___(Name)___ and I require of you a seven-fold return of all you have stolen. I say this in Jesus' name and by His strength, power and authority! Hallelujah and Amen!

Day 30
Rivers Of Living Water

> *Just jump in today and let the river of God carry you where He is going.*

Ezek. 47:5, 9 *"Again he measured a thousand; and it was a river that I could not ford, for the water had risen, enough water to swim in, a river that could not be forded... And it will come about that every living creature which swarms in every place where the river goes, will live. And there will be very many fish, for these waters go there, and the others become fresh; so **everything will live where the river goes.**"*

John 7:38 *"'He who believes in Me, as the Scripture said, 'From his innermost being shall flow **rivers of living water.**'"*

Isa. 35:4-6 *"Say to those with anxious heart, 'Take courage, fear not. Behold, your God will come with vengeance; the recompense of God will come, but He will save you.' Then the eyes of the blind will be opened, and the ears of the deaf will be unstopped. Then the lame will leap like a deer. And the tongue of the dumb will shout for joy. For **waters will break forth in the wilderness, and streams in the desert.**"*

Deep river waters. "A river that could not be forded." "Enough water to swim in." The source of Ezekiel's river was the temple of God. In John, the Revelator's account, the source of the river of life is God's throne (see Rev. 22). Regardless of the typology, the Source of life is the Lord, Himself, and the place where His presence dwells. When the river of His Spirit flows into our lives, He desires for it to rise and flow out of our lives. Jesus declared the living water would flow from our innermost being. Can you fathom the great truth that He proclaimed to us? As we worship and come before the presence of God, the river of heaven comes into our deepest places, fills us up, and flows out of us becoming His life to others. Think of it: God's life source is in you! And the promise the prophet proclaimed was that *"...everything will live where the river goes."*

Suppose that you could water the wilderness, desolate places of your children's lives with His healing streams. Their desert of devastation would become a lush garden. What a wonderful, awesome thing that would be!

Rivers Of Living Water

The truth is that you can do that very thing! When you speak life-giving words to your son/daughter, the river is flowing. You don't have to quote scripture or say "Thus sayeth the Lord..." You just let the river of life flow however He desires to flow out of you. The thing about "rivers to swim in" is that the swimmer does not control the course of the waters. When it comes to our kids, it is hard to let go of the control. Yet, when we yield ourselves to Him and become a swimmer, He will take us and use us for His glory. I suggest that you:

Just jump in today and let the river of God carry you where He is going.

You will be blessed and surprised how His river of life will flow through you to help transform your children's desert. Sometimes, God just wants us to say an encouraging word or maybe a word of peace to them. When we let His river of life flow out of us, the words are sometimes so simple. "It will be okay. You're going to do good on your test." "Don't worry, God is with you." "God will take care of it. Try not to be afraid." "God's on your side." "I believe in you; you can do it." All of these are examples of words of life that He had me say to my kids. My mind was telling me the opposite. My mind told me that they didn't deserve a break because of their poor choices. My mind was saying, "God is gong to make you pay for this! I am afraid for you that trouble is coming if you don't turn it around!" But, out of my innermost being, the river of life would flow. These words made the opening for the miraculous. Isaiah said, *"**Then** the eyes of the blind will be opened..."* (Isa. 35:5). When? After the **saying** to the anxious heart, the miracles were released. Life came to the wilderness.

Today, try letting the river of life flow through you in the little things. Bit by bit, the desert in your son's or daughter's life will begin to bloom.

Prayer:

Father, I recognize You and Your presence today. I invite You, Holy Spirit, to fill me and flow out of me. Please let me know where You want to go and how You want to flow into my child's life. Use me however you choose to bring Your life to his/her life. Thank You for

Your grace – for not giving any of us what we truly deserve. In Jesus' name, Amen.

Proclamation:

I speak to the dry wilderness places in ___ (Name's) ___ life and say, "Be broken up! Receive the Living Waters! Receive life! Your God is coming and He will save you!"

Day 31
The Moment of Truth

> *The loving truth of the Artist is coming to lift the veil from the eyes of your child.*

John 4:16-19, 39 *"He said to her, 'Go call your husband, and come here.' The woman answered and said, 'I have no husband.' Jesus said to her, 'You have well said, 'I have no husband;' for you have had five husbands, and the one whom you now have is not your husband. This you have said truly.' The woman said to Him, 'Sir, I perceive that You are a prophet'...And from that city many of the Samaritans believed in Him because of the word of the woman who testified, 'He told me all the things that I have done.'"*

Eph. 1:18 *"I pray that the eyes of your heart may be enlightened, so that you may know what is the hope of His calling..."*

Everyone has their moment of truth. There comes a day when the Lord walks right into the middle of things and pulls back the cover. The actual meaning of the word revelation is "to unveil." Can you imagine the moment when the artist lifts the draping from the canvas of his painting? It is the unveiling or the revelation of his creation. Your son or daughter is like that work of art – a beautiful masterpiece hidden under a cover of deception. The Lord has let you have an early glimpse of the glory of this painting because, other than Him, you are the primary investor. You have seen in your own heart the design of the Lord. You know how it looks under that cover. You watched as the Artist painted the canvas with brilliant indescribable colors. Through the years, you saw the various techniques He used to tell His story on the canvas of your son's or daughter's life. He never intended to cover this art work.

Yet, somehow, the drapery of deception came over the beautiful life of your child. And, now, you may wonder if you will ever see the unveiling. Just as Jesus walked out of His way to meet the Samaritan woman by the well, He will meet your child where he/she may be. He will speak the truth into the midst of the deception. He will prove to your wayward one that He knows his/her hidden sins. The revelation that He knows the truth about us and still loves us enough to come after us is freeing.

The Moment of Truth

The loving truth of the Artist is coming to lift the veil from the eyes of your child.

No one is more tender with a masterpiece than the Master...the Creator...the One who dreamed the design in the beginning.

What is your job at this critical moment? You're not an ordinary onlooker in the crowd. You are a personal friend of the Artist, Himself. There's really not much for you to do, except to be available to Him. And, when the unveiling happens, then what? The painting will go home with the highest bidder. I think that is you.

When the truth comes to set your son or daughter free, he/she may not literally go home with you. Yet, you will be carrying this moment of truth in your heart forever. Until then, be available to the Artist. He won't let you miss the unveiling.

Prayer:

Father, I ask You to give me a fresh look at Your design for my child's life. I am available to You today for however You would want to use me. Please speak the truth to___(Name)___ and lift the deception from his/her eyes. In Jesus' name, Amen. Be Glorified in my son's/daughter's life!

Proclamation:

In Jesus' name, I speak the word of truth: "Be unveiled. Let the deception be lifted right now. Let the Spirit of revelation open your eyes to God and His design for your life!"

Day 32
Possess The Gates Of Your Enemy

> *The fortified strongholds of Satan will no longer hold your offspring captive, but, rather, they shall plunder and possess that which has plundered and possessed them.*

Gen. 22:14-18 *"And Abraham called the name of that place 'The Lord Will Provide' as it is said to this day, 'In the mount of the Lord, it will be provided.' Then the angel of the Lord called to Abraham a **second time** from heaven, and said, 'By Myself I have sworn,' declares the Lord, 'because you have done this thing, and have not withheld your son, your only son, indeed I will greatly bless you, and I will greatly multiply your seed as the stars of the heavens, and as the sand which is on the seashore; and **your seed shall possess the gate of their enemies**. And in your seed all the nations of the earth shall be blessed because you have obeyed My voice.'"*

We do the best we can to obey the Lord's voice when it comes to our kids. We try to point them to God, His Word, and His ways. There comes a critical time when, like Abraham, we will have our faith tested. The agony that Abraham experienced as he climbed the mountain with his son, Isaac, is something I am sure you can relate to. God had a plan to strengthen Abraham's faith in His promises. He did this by testing Abraham's obedience. He required the sacrifice of his son. God asked him to go to the mountain and worship by building an altar with Isaac as the offering. Just as the knife was raised, the voice of the Lord thundered from heaven, **the second time.** The ram was provided and Isaac was untied from the altar.

Today the Lord is asking you for a sacrifice. He wants you to ascend into worship and bring your child with you in your heart. He wants you to worship Him even though you cannot see the provision. He is asking you not to withhold your son or daughter from Him. You may say, "I have given my child to Him. I don't withhold him/her from the Lord." Yet, if you are so down, discouraged, or disappointed that you cannot worship Him unreservedly, then maybe you are holding on too tightly to your precious one. It was in the mount of the Lord (the place of worship) that the substitute was provided. It was in the place of ultimate sacrifice that the voice of the Lord came thundering from

84

heaven – the second time. The first time was the call to worship and obedience. The second time was the confirmation of the promise and the return of his son.

When you obediently give the sacrifice of praise to the Lord, the heavens will open and you, too, will hear His promise confirmed to you again. Just as He told Abraham, *"Your seed shall possess the gates of their enemies."*

The fortified strongholds of Satan will no longer hold your offspring captive, but, rather, they shall plunder and possess that which has plundered and possessed them.

Your worshipful obedience releases the provision for your child's deliverance. It also opens your heart to hear His voice again. The promise to you still remains the same; and the power to possess the enemy's gates belongs to your offspring. The trip up the mountain of sacrificial worship may be painful, but just remember, the provision and the promise will be there waiting.

Prayer:

Lord, today, I bring You the sacrifice of worship. As I place my child upon Your altar, I ask You to open my eyes to see Your provision and restoration and open my ears to hear Your voice. In Your Name, Amen.

Proclamation:

Because of the provision of Calvary's sacrifice, I stand upon and declare the promise over my children: "You shall possess the gates of your enemies!"

Day 33
"I Am Willing!"

> He isn't planning calamity and catastrophe; He is planning a homecoming.

Matt. 8:2-3 *"And behold a leper came to Him, and bowed down to Him, saying, 'Lord if You are willing, You can make me clean.' And He stretched out His hand and touched him, saying, 'I am willing; be cleansed.' And immediately his leprosy was cleansed."*

Prov. 13:12 *"Hope deferred makes the heart sick, but desire fulfilled is a tree of life."*

Jer. 29:11 *"'For I know the plans that I have for you,' declares the Lord, 'plans for welfare and not for calamity to give you a future and a hope.'"*

Jer. 31:17 *"'And there is hope for your future,' declares the Lord, 'and your children shall return to their own territory.'"*

In the Word of God, leprosy is a typology of sin. It was an incurable and highly contagious disease which would eat away the flesh of the afflicted person. Because of its unmerciful affects and risks, the victim would be isolated in order not to infect others. If a leper did enter the community, he was required by the Law to shout "Unclean!" in order to give fair warning to anyone in his path. The disease, like sin, was a hopeless condition. Only a miracle touch from Jesus could heal it and restore the person to health. Jesus was not afraid of the awful disease. It was not a problem to Him to touch the unclean person. To the seeking leper, He was the only hope. When the leper asked if He would be willing to heal him, Jesus unreservedly declared, *"I am willing."*

Your son's or daughter's sin sickness is not hopeless. It isn't beyond His reach. Even if others have rejected and isolated your child, He has not. His heart's cry to your beloved son/daughter is "I am willing! I will touch what no one else will dare to touch. I will look at what others cannot bare to gaze upon. I will heal you and make you like new."

Do you know why you need this hope today? You need hope today because of your heart sickness. When hope has been delayed, the heart becomes sick. It is that ache which seems to never go away that

86

"I Am Willing!"

is the symptom which points to the hopelessness. I can see Jesus reaching into your heart with His healing touch right now. He is putting a seed of hope in the aching place. As it grows, you will begin to truly realize that what He has in mind for you and your children is a good future.

He isn't planning calamity and catastrophe;
He is planning a homecoming.

Receive His hope into your heart and be healed. He is willing to heal and deliver your child and He is willing to heal you!

Prayer:

Thank You, Jesus, for being willing to heal us. Please touch the places in my son/daughter that no one else will touch. I ask You for full restoration and newness of life for both of us. Place Your seed of hope in me today and cause me to see the future that You have planned. In Your Name, Amen.

Proclamation:

_____(Name)_____ is healed of all sin sickness and delivered from all of its effects by the blood of Jesus! I am filled with hope because He will not delay His plans for our lives. We have a future and a hope! Hallelujah!

Day 34
"Sweet Hour Of Prayer"

> *Sometimes, the best thing you can do for yourself and your children is to withdraw into the secret place, rest awhile, and pray.*

Matt. 11:28-29 *"'Come to Me, all who are weary and heavy-laden, and I will give you rest. Take My yoke upon you, and learn from Me, for I am gentle and humble in heart; and you shall find rest for your souls. For My yoke is easy, and My load is light.'"*

Matt. 14:23 *"And after He had sent the multitudes away, He went up to the mountain by Himself to pray; and when it was evening, He was there alone."*

When I was a child, I would hear my mother in the other room quietly humming the old hymn, "Sweet Hour of Prayer." I can remember the feeling of safety and peace that accompanied her song. She never said much about Jesus to me, but her life was a prayer. She taught me the value of quiet and solitude by the way she went about her daily tasks around our house. I grew up with an understanding that being alone for awhile can be a good thing. If I misbehaved and needed to "think about" what I had done, she would give me a spanking and send me to a certain corner in our hallway to "think." I am pretty sure that I learned about prayer in that corner. If I cried and threw a fit, she would just make me sit there longer. If I talked or played with my cousin, Steve, (who was usually "thinking" in the opposite corner), the time would be extended even more. So, as I sat there, I learned about quieting myself. That is really one of the key ingredients to prayer.

Many years later when things went wrong with my daughters, I found myself, from time to time, humming the old song:

> *Sweet hour of prayer! sweet hour of prayer!*
> *that calls me from a world of care,*
> *and bids me at my Father's throne*
> *make all my wants and wishes known.*
> *In seasons of distress and grief,*
> *my soul has often found relief,*
> *and oft escaped the tempter's snare*
> *by thy return, sweet hour of prayer!*

"Sweet Hour Of Prayer"

Sweet hour of prayer! sweet hour of prayer!
the joys I feel, the bliss I share
of those whose anxious spirits burn
with strong desires for thy return!
With such I hasten to the place
where God my Savior shows his face,
and gladly take my station there,
and wait for thee, sweet hour of prayer!

Sweet hour of prayer! sweet hour of prayer!
thy wings shall my petition bear
to him whose truth and faithfulness
engage the waiting soul to bless.
And since he bids me seek his face,
believe his word, and trust his grace,
I'll cast on him my every care,
and wait for thee, sweet hour of prayer!

Today is a time to quiet yourself and enter into His rest. When Jesus had finished ministering to the multitudes, He would often withdraw to the mountain and pray. He knew the secret of solitude. It was after one such occasion, that He walked upon the waves of the storm and saved His floundering disciples.

Sometimes, the best thing you can do for
yourself and your children is to withdraw
into the secret place, rest awhile, and pray.

From there, you will gain new perspective, new strength and supernatural strategy for the storm.

Prayer:

Today, Lord, I rest in You. I quiet my soul and lean into Your arms of love. I receive Your peace and quiet as a gift from heaven. In Jesus' name, Amen.

"Sweet Hour of Prayer" courtesy of HymnSite.com Home

Day 35
Above All Else!

> **Let every tormenting thought bow to His Lordship and be taken into captivity by Calvary's victory.**

2 Cor. 10:3-5 *"For though we walk in the flesh, we do not war according to the flesh, for the weapons of our warfare are not of the flesh, but divinely powerful for the destruction of fortresses. We are destroying speculations and every lofty thing raised up against the knowledge of God, and we are taking every thought captive to the obedience of Christ."*

Josh. 1:8 *"' This book of the law shall not depart from your mouth, but you shall meditate on it day and night, so that you may be careful to do according to all that is written in it; for then you will make your way prosperous, and then you will have success.'"*

"A penny for your thoughts." The old expression is supposed to cause us to realize that we are staring off into space, possibly daydreaming or captivated by worry. It symbolically indicates that our thoughts and attention have value. We could have been in a conversation with someone and somehow our minds floated far away down another road. You know what it's like, right? You may have been out to dinner with friends or doing your job at the office and your mind went to your backslidden child. Lots of times your imaginations can simply run wild. You may begin to speculate about where he/she may be or what he/she may be doing. It is amazing how the thoughts of this one can overtake whatever you are doing, and stop you cold. I know that sometimes my family members and dearest friends would feel hurt that my attention was diverted again and again. It would sadden me that my wandering thoughts and preoccupation with my daughter would affect my other precious relationships.

Then, one day, the Lord showed me how He felt. He showed me that He, too, was hurting. He could hear my heart and my thoughts. He could see that it was my daughter and her problems that dominated my mind. She was the priority above Him. I had exalted her to a place of preeminence on the throne of my heart. She didn't want that place; she actually wished that I wouldn't be so focused on her. My obsession made her feel uncomfortable and crowded.

Above All Else!

I realized that the Lord was my "Joshua" and He desired to conquer the land of my heart and mind with His great love. The reality was that the greatest battlefield was in my mind. He wanted to displace the enemies of worry and fear with peace and joy. The Holy Spirit began to teach me that by meditating (purposefully choosing to think and concentrate) on His Word, the strongholds in my mind would be destroyed and He would be enthroned in my life. The old thinking patterns had to be brought down low under His Lordship. As I began to yield to Him and let Him change my thoughts by His Word, the priority of His presence was established. As I gazed upon Him, I came to know that no one and nothing is worthy of such adoration and uninterrupted attention and focus.

What is it that captivates your thoughts? What do you find yourself thinking about the most? Is it your son or daughter? If it is, then maybe he/she has been elevated to the place of His throne in your heart. The Lord Jesus desires to take this prominent place in you so that His kingdom can come and rule over all. The wayward child has had the center of your attention for way too long. The truth is that he/she really doesn't want it and He really does. Today, as you worship Him, allow Him to take His rightful place above all else.

Let every tormenting thought bow to His Lordship
and be taken into captivity by Calvary's victory.

Begin to consciously choose to meditate upon Him and His Word. If you do, your way will be prosperous and you will have success.

Prayer:

Lord Jesus, please forgive me for placing the priority of my thoughts on my son/daughter. I want to exalt You to the highest place of honor. Please, come as my Joshua, and capture my heart completely. In Your Name, Amen.

Proclamation:

Right now, I speak to my thoughts, imaginations and speculations: "I call you into divine order and under His rule and reign. I take you captive and hold you in check to the Lordship of Jesus!"

Day 36
The Awakening

Your child cannot outrun God!	**Gen. 28:11** *"And he came to a certain place and spent the night there, because the sun had set..."*
	Gen. 28:12 *"And he had a dream, and behold, a ladder was set on the earth with its top reaching to heaven; and behold, the angels of God were ascending and descending on it."*

Gen. 28:16-17 *"Then Jacob awoke from his sleep and said, 'Surely the Lord is in this place, and I did not know it!' And he was afraid and said, 'How awesome is this place! This is none other than the house of God, and this is the gate of heaven!'"*

Many times our children run away from the purposes of God for their lives. Their fear of facing the consequences of their choices drives them to try and escape **from** God instead of running **to** Him. Jacob ran away because of his fear of Esau's wrath. He had stolen his brother's birthright and he knew that it was sin.

Sometimes your son/daughter may be running from the possible consequences of their sin just as much as they are running from God. This may cause you to feel that he/she is being irresponsible and insensitive to you and your family. This may be true, but there also may be a fear factor. The fear of the consequences may be blinding him/her to the truth of God's love. When we cannot see any way out of a terrible situation because of the blinders of fear, we may make unwise decisions in order to get immediate relief. Your son/daughter cannot see the way out. So, he/she runs.

In spite of the reason for running, God is in pursuit. He will allow him/her to run until he/she collapses from exhaustion.

Your child cannot outrun God!

Just as Jacob had to stop running at a certain place, so does your son/daughter have to stop running. It was there, where Jacob slept, that God opened heaven and visited him. God will take full advantage of the slightest opportunity. He knows the exact location where your child will come to the end of his/her strength. He is already there waiting to open heaven and extend the ladder of access. Jacob had a divine appointment and didn't know it. He ran straight into the gateway of heaven when he laid his head down that night.

Your son or daughter cannot miss his/her meeting with God. There is no place to run that would be out of His reach. The love of God is limitless and it has no bounds. He can open heaven over a bar, a brothel, a drug house, or a back alley. Darkness and devils do not hinder the Lord's ability to reach your child. When he/she runs out of options, He will be there with the way out. The way out of any impossible bondage is ... up! Jacob discovered the gateway of heaven even though he was in the midst of deception and rebellion. Don't be discouraged by your son's or daughter's distance from you. Don't let the location of his/her heart cause you distress. There is no place that is unreachable to God and His love. Heaven's ladder is extended right now in whatever place he/she may be. Just as Jacob was awakened by His awesome presence and power – so it shall be with your child. He/She is going to wake up to realize that He is there.

Prayer:

Lord, please open heaven over my child. Cause him/her to awaken and recognize Your awesome presence and purpose for his/her life. In Jesus' name, Amen.

Proclamation:

In Jesus' name, I speak to the spirit of slumber over my child and say, "Be gone! Be removed!" To ____(Name)____, I say, "Awaken to the Lord and His plan for your life. I call you out of darkness and into His wonderful light."

Day 37
Commitment

By giving Him **all** the glory for their successes and trusting Him to take their sins upon Himself, we can be free.

Isa. 45:11 *"Thus says the Lord, the Holy One of Israel, and his Maker: 'Ask Me about the things to come concerning My sons, and you shall commit to Me, the work of My hands.'"*

Ps. 90:15-17 *"Make us glad according to the days Thou has afflicted us, and the years we have seen evil. Let Thy work appear to Thy servants, and Thy majesty to their children. And let the favor of the Lord our God be upon us; and do confirm for us the work of our hands; yes, confirm* (give permanence to) *the work of our hands."*

As our children are growing up, we say prayers asking for God's blessings to be upon them. We ask Him to guard and keep them from falling and to give them favor. We pray for ourselves to have wisdom to know what to do or say to train them. Secretly, we hope that they will make us proud to be their parents. We have to be honest and admit that we don't want our kids to make us look bad. If they mess up, part of the pain we feel is our own hurt pride. Their backslidings are a reflection of us and our failures in parenting. At least, that is how it feels.

When our kids make straight A's, make the winning touchdowns, or are picked for the star roles in the school play, it is easy to pat ourselves on the back and take credit for their success. Similarly, if they are caught shoplifting, doing drugs, or being sexually promiscuous, we find it easy to take the blame. This can be especially devastating if we have spent too much time bragging in previous days. The higher that we exalt our kids – the further down they must fall.

Either one of these scenarios is rooted in pride. Pride is one of the biggest traps the devil can set for us. The element of ownership becomes the true issue. Whose son or daughter is he/she? Have we truly committed our kids to Him?

*By giving Him **all** the glory for their successes and trusting Him to take their sins upon Himself, we can be free.*

Commitment

When they are small children, we must take responsibility for their actions and yet keep in mind that they are loaned to us by God. However, a day comes when He asks for us to turn them completely back over to Him. It is hard to realize that our work is done. It's as if He says, "Thanks for all you've done, but I will take it from here."

Maybe you feel like I did. I wanted to tell Him how He should handle my daughter. I gave Him advice as to what she needed. I made suggestions to Him for how to bring her into breakthrough and deliverance. I kept Him informed of how much time was being wasted. Finally, I came to understand that He didn't need my help! All He wanted was my commitment to leave her in His hands and my agreement with His way of doing things.

God gave me the most wonderful privilege that He also has given to you. He gave me full and unlimited access to His throne room and permission to ask Him for a status report on my daughter. Even though my daughter would lie to me, He would tell me the truth. Even though she didn't tell me where she was, He would show me. Sometimes, He would not disclose her actual location, but He would show me that she was safe. If you will come and ask Him, He will do the same for you.

Why not ask Him to show you what He is doing in your child's life? **God wants you to be in the loop.** He knows that you can be trusted with His special treasure. After all, didn't He pick you to be the parent in the beginning?

Prayer:

Father, please forgive me for my pride. Lord, I repent for all the times I secretly took credit for my children's successes. I repent also for trying to carry their sins and pay for their mistakes. You are their only Savior. I commit my children into Your hands. I ask You, Lord, to reveal to me what You are doing so that I can agree with Your plans in prayer. In Jesus' name, Amen.

Proclamation:

____(Name)____, I commit you into God's hands. I release you from my plans for you and commit you to His.

Day 38
The Secret Place

> *The hiding place of His presence is available to you at any time and at any place.*

Ps. 91:1-2 *"He who dwells in the secret place of the Most High will abide in the shadow of the Almighty. I will say to the Lord, 'my refuge and my fortress, my God in whom I trust.'"*

Ps. 27:5 *"For in the day of trouble, He will conceal me in His shelter. In the secret place of His tent, He will hide me..."*

Ps. 31:20 *"Thou dost hide them in the secret place of Thy presence from the conspiracies of man; Thou dost keep them secretly in a shelter from the strife of tongues."*

Ps. 32:7 *"Thou art my hiding place; Thou dost preserve me from trouble; Thou dost surround me with songs of deliverance."*

Luke 1:34-35, 37 *"And Mary said to the angel, 'How can this be...?' and the angel answered her and said to her, 'The Holy Spirit will come upon you, and the power of the Most High will overshadow you... For nothing will be impossible with God.'"*

Did you ever just wish you could hide? Have you ever thought that you would give anything if you could disappear? When your backslidden child is the topic of discussion, you feel so vulnerable and exposed. Gossip is a cruel and merciless tool of Satan. It is too bad that many church folks spend valuable time exchanging tales (sometimes cloaked as prayer requests) instead of simply praying. Too often, our backslidden kids do not find the church to be a safe place. Not only can the church be unsafe for our kids, but it can also feel unsafe to us. Rumors may fly through the air like sharp arrows.

It is at these times that we may find ourselves hiding behind our walls of pretense. We may say to the inquiring person, "Oh, he isn't well today." Or, "She had to work; she really wanted to be here." We may find ourselves trying to cover up for our kids in order to protect them from people's opinions and judgments. When this happens, we are positioning ourselves to become our kids' shield and salvation.

The solution is not to drop out of church. The same thing can happen

96

in our neighborhood or even among our relatives. People are going to talk whether they are Christians or not. It is simply carnal nature in action. There is a place to hide from such talk, gossip, and slander.

The hiding place of His presence is available to you at any time and at any place.

Regardless of the insults of men, you can be sheltered in the shadow of your Father. If a bully was picking on a small child and the child's father came onto the scene, the bully would immediately back down. Even as the shadow of the father's presence approached, it would cover the small child and intimidate the bully. Likewise, when you are being "bullied" by the words of men, run into your Father's shadow. You can hide in the secret place of His presence.

Can you imagine the gossip that must have gone around Nazareth about Mary when she became pregnant? She must have had to find the secret place time and time again. She must have remembered the angel's answer to her question regarding her ability to conceive: *"The Holy Spirit will overshadow you."* She remembered that there was a secret place where miracles could happen. In that hiding place, the impossible became possible.

When you come into His presence, bring your child with you in your heart. Let His shadow be the shelter and refuge from every tongue. In that place, the angels sing songs of deliverance that will absolutely drown out every sound. You could never find a better hiding place. Miracles happen there! Whether you are at church, your family gathering, or the neighborhood block party, you are covered. And, that's a great feeling!

Prayer:

Lord Jesus, thank You for casting Your shadow over us. Hide us from all gossip and slander and let us hear the angels sing! Hallelujah!

Proclamation:

In Jesus' name, I take authority over every slanderous word and judgment. I break their power by His Word and blood. I say that these weapons will no longer prosper against me or my children. I release His words of blessing and forgiveness to those who have spoken against us. We are free!

Day 39
Forgiveness

| Fuel your faith by releasing forgiveness. | Matt. 18:21-22 *"Then Peter came and said to Him: 'Lord, how often shall my brother sin against me and I forgive him? Up to seven times?' And Jesus said to him, 'I do not say to you, up to seven times, but up to seventy times seven!'"* |

Matt. 6:12 *"'And forgive us our debts, as we also have forgiven our debtors.'"*

Luke 23:34 *"But Jesus was saying, 'Father, forgive them; for they do not know what they are doing.'"*

Over and over again we forgive our children for their sins against us. There are times when bitterness and unforgiveness try to set in and harden our hearts; but our love conquers it. There are times that we may say to ourselves, "That's the last time he/she will hurt me like that. I'll just write him/her off. If I don't have to be around him/her, then it won't hurt so bad." But who are we kidding? The love for our children is bigger than the pain and hurt.

Each time that you choose to forgive and let unconditional love triumph, there is new ground taken in the battle. Your forgiveness is a reminder to your son or daughter of the love of God. It is also a reminder to Satan that you are not giving up! **Every time that you forgive you are standing in a place of faith that pleases God.** Faith says, "I believe the truth about my child and therefore I release him/her from this action that hurt me."

As Jesus hung upon the cross, He looked down through the ages and forgave you for all of the times you would sin against Him and reject His love. He saw you with eyes of unconditional love and eyes of faith. When you were against Him, He was for you. When you were making choices in opposition to His plan for your life, He made the Love choice of Calvary for you.

In the same way, when you suffer pain from the
wounds inflicted by your child's backsliding,
fuel your faith by releasing forgiveness.

Forgiveness

Choose to look past your suffering to view the fulfillment of God's promise. Your son/daughter will never truly know and understand the extent of your suffering. But, they will know and realize the extent of your love.

Forgiveness and faith mingle together to bring us to a place of forgetting. God has chosen to not only forgive, but to forget. Once a sinner repents, the sin is never mentioned again. It is as if it never happened!

I can still remember some of the backslidden days of my children, but I have made the love choice of forgiveness. Bit by bit, the memories are healed and begin to fade. As you forgive your child for their sins against you, the fuel of faith will ignite the fire and zeal of your heart with new hope. You will see past the current behaviors and gain a glimpse of better days to come. In the light of Calvary's victory the bitter memories will begin to grow dim in the glorious presence of the One who forgave you.

Prayer:

Father, please forgive ____(Name)____. I forgive him/her for the hurts that he/she has caused me. Please fuel my faith today with the power that flows from this forgiveness. I appropriate the blood of Jesus to cleanse and wash me from all the wounding. Thank You for the cross. In His Marvelous Name, Amen.

Proclamation:

____(Name)____, I forgive you! I release you from everything that you have done to hurt me. May the power of this forgiveness overtake you today with God's amazing love and grace.

Day 40
A Day To Declare The Word

Your words are powerful and carry with them the life of God. When you agree with His word and declare it over your children, His creative power begins to move over the darkness of their lives and releases His light. Today is a day to take every opportunity to practice speaking forth the promises of God. You will sense His anointing and experience a personal breakthrough. There is great power in agreement. These are a few of my favorites that I use to declare over my children. You may want to add some of your own. Have a fruitful and blessed day.

Isa. 59:21 – Isa. 60:1-2 *"'As for Me, this is My covenant with them,' says the Lord: 'My Spirit which is upon you, and My words which I have put in your mouth, shall not depart from your mouth, nor from the mouth of your offspring, nor from the mouth of your offspring's offspring,' says the Lord, 'from now and forever.' Arise, shine; for your light has come, and the glory of the Lord has risen upon you. For behold, darkness will cover the earth, and deep darkness the peoples; but the Lord will rise upon you, and His glory will appear upon you."*

Ps. 103:17-18 *"But the lovingkindness of the Lord is from everlasting to everlasting on those who fear Him, and His righteousness to children's children, to those who keep His covenant, and who remember His precepts to do them."*

Isa. 8:18 *"Behold, I and the children whom the Lord has given me are for signs and wonders in Israel from the Lord of hosts, who dwells on Mount Zion."*

Isa. 54:13 *"And all your sons will be taught of the Lord; and the well-being of your sons will be great."*

Joel 2:28-29 *"'And it will come about after this that I will pour out My Spirit on all mankind; and your sons and daughters will prophesy, your old men will dream dreams, your young men will see visions. And even on the male and female servants I will pour out My Spirit in those days.'"*

A Day To Declare The Word

Isa. 61:6-7, 9 *"But you will be called the priests of the Lord; you will be spoken of as ministers of our God. You will eat the wealth of nations, and in their riches you will boast. Instead of your shame you will have a double portion, and instead of humiliation they will shout for joy over their portion. Therefore, they will possess a double portion in their land, everlasting joy will be theirs...Then their offspring will be known among the nations, and their descendants in the midst of the peoples. All who see them will recognize them because they are the offspring whom the Lord has blessed."*

Isa. 54:17 *"'No weapon that is formed against you shall prosper; and every tongue that accuses you in judgment you will condemn. This is the heritage of the servants of the Lord, and their vindication is from Me,' declares the Lord."*

ABOUT LANORA VAN ARSDALL

LaNora Van Arsdall has been given a mandate from the Lord to stir up hunger for Him in the hearts of His people. Her intimate, personal walk with the Lord is evident in her ministry. Her apostolic anointing and prophetic revelation of the Word bring breakthrough to individuals and churches. Lives are changed as His impartation and anointing flow through her. She is the author of **Breakthrough Anointing –** *Divine Strategies for a Life of Spiritual Power.*

In her 32 years of ministry, LaNora has pastored, served as the Arizona State Representative for Spiritual Warfare Network, and served on the staff of Iverna Tompkins Ministry. She currently serves on the board of Gatekeepers International Prophetic Network and on the leadership team of Fountain of Life Fellowship, Mesa, Arizona. In 2000, with the blessing and impartation of Dr. Fuchsia (Mom) Pickett, she launched FountainGate Ministries International which has a dual vision of uniting ministries and pastors and transforming cities through presence evangelism. FountainGate Ministries is the apostolic covering for her local church, Fountain of Life Fellowship in Mesa, Arizona and for Freedom Fellowship in Tucson, Arizona.

LaNora resides in Mesa, Arizona. She has two daughters, Melanie and Kari. Melanie and her husband, Daniel, have five children. Kari and her husband, Tim, have two children and are pastors of Fountain of Life Fellowship in Mesa, Arizona.

*To schedule speaking engagements
or to order LaNora's books, contact:*

LaNora Van Arsdall
FountainGate Ministries Intl.
P. O. Box 1333
Gilbert, AZ 85299-1333

Phone: 1-877-658-8388
Website: www.FountainGateIntl.org
E-mail: FountainGate@FountainGateIntl.com

Breakthrough Anointing
Divine Strategies for a Life of Spiritual Power

40 Days to Freedom
*Prayers and Proclamations to Call Your
Backslidden Children Into Their Destiny*

NOTES

NOTES

NOTES

NOTES

NOTES

NOTES